W9-BAN-471

THE MODERN
SHORT STORY

ALSO BY H. E. BATES

Novels

THE TWO SISTERS
CHARLOTTE'S ROW
THE POACHER
SPELLA HO
THE CRUISE OF THE BREADWINNER
THE JACARANDA TREE
LOVE FOR LYDIA
THE SLEEPLESS MOON
THE DARLING BUDS OF MAY
A BREATH OF FRENCH AIR
A CROWN OF WILD MYRTLE
THE DISTANT HORNS OF SUMMER

CATHERINE FOSTER
THE FALLOW LAND
A HOUSE OF WOMEN
FAIR STOOD THE WIND FOR FRANCE
THE PURPLE PLAIN
THE SCARLET SWORD
THE FEAST OF JULY
WHEN THE GREEN WOODS LAUGH
THE DAY OF THE TORTOISE
OH! TO BE IN ENGLAND
A MOMENT IN TIME
A LITTLE OF WHAT YOU FANCY

Short Stories

DAY'S END
THE BLACK BOXER
CUT AND COME AGAIN
THE FLYING COAT
THE BRIDE COMES TO EVENSFORD
COLONEL JULIAN
THE WATERCRESS GIRL
DEATH OF A HUNTSMAN
THE GOLDEN ORIOLE
THE WILD CHERRY TREE

SEVEN TALES AND ALEXANDER
THE WOMAN WHO HAD IMAGINATION
SOMETHING SHORT AND SWEET
THE BEAUTY OF THE DEAD
DEAR LIFE
THE DAFFODIL SKY
NOW SLEEPS THE CRIMSON PETAL
THE NATURE OF LOVE
AN ASPIDISTRA IN BABYLON
THE FOUR BEAUTIES

THE SONG OF THE WREN

Drama

THE DAY OF GLORY

Essays

FLOWERS AND FACES
DOWN THE RIVER
THE HEART OF THE COUNTRY
THE COUNTRY HEART

THROUGH THE WOODS
THE SEASONS AND THE GARDENER
O! MORE THAN HAPPY COUNTRYMAN
THE COUNTRY OF WHITE CLOVER

EDWARD GARNETT: A MEMOIR

Collections of Short Stories

THIRTY TALES

THE FABULOUS MRS V.
COUNTRY TALES
MY UNCLE SILAS
(*Illustrated by Edward Ardizzone*)

THE WEDDING PARTY
SEVEN BY FIVE
SUGAR FOR THE HORSE
(*Illustrated by Edward Ardizzone*)

Autobiography

THE VANISHED WORLD   THE BLOSSOMING WORLD

As 'Flying Officer X'

THE GREATEST PEOPLE IN THE WORLD   HOW SLEEP THE BRAVE

For Children

ACHILLES THE DONKEY   ACHILLES AND DIANA

THE
MODERN SHORT STORY

A CRITICAL SURVEY

by

H. E. BATES

THE WRITER, INC.

PUBLISHERS

BOSTON, MASSACHUSETTS

Published in the United States by
The Writer, Inc. 1972

© 1972 by Evensford Productions Ltd

REPRINTED 1976

LCCCN: 79-187587

ISBN 0–87116–070–6

CONTENTS

v

PREFACE TO NEW EDITION

THE realm of prophecy and that of betting on racehorses have at least two things in common: whereas both are a mug's game the participants in each are always promising to learn by experience but rarely do.

When at the conclusion of *The Modern Short Story* in 1941 I prophesied that if the war then in progress produced nothing else in the way of literature it would certainly provide a rich crop of short stories, I did not for one moment believe that the statement was by any means a rash one. On the contrary, I felt it to be self-evident that at such a time of dislocation, excitement and widening of experience in all manner of directions and for all manner of people, a vast amount of material, inestimable, as I saw it, in its value for short story writers both established and new, would inevitably be thrown up. The bombing of London, the war in all its theatres, in the air, on the sea, in the desert, in the jungle: all this offered, or seemed to offer, a rich and exciting vein of experience such as the comparatively humdrum days of peace could never match. Out of it, I consequently thought, must come short stories: my bet being on short stories rather than novels for the good reason that at such a time of crisis the physical effort of producing the shorter form must inevitably make it the more probable and acceptable medium of the two.

In all this I made several mistakes, having forgotten, for example, the fundamental principle that because a short story is short it is not therefore easier to write than a novel, ten, twenty or thirty times its length—the exact reverse being in fact the truth. I had also forgotten another truth, namely, that mere experience of itself cannot automatically create a work of art, since in the last crucial essence all art is a physical act. All the fine dreams, the sublimest excursions of the mind, the most exciting of experiences, the most beautiful of thoughts are as nothing until the act of transmuting them into physical terms has been accomplished. Until the writer has put pen to paper, the artist his paint to canvas, the sculptor his tools to

7

wood, stone and marble, the composer his notes to the score, there is, in fact, nothing.

I had also allowed myself to be misled in yet another direction. I had supposed that the aftermath of war would find expression, after the long dark tragic years, in light and joy. It never occurred to me, even remotely, that it might well express itself in a sourness even darker. Of course the virtues of hindsight are legion. We could not possibly know, in 1941, what course or courses literature would seek out for itself, or be seduced into, in the fifties, sixties, or, Heaven help us, the seventies. We had no way of foreseeing the era of the Angry Young Men, the Permissive Society or the Parade of Pornography.

All this, however, duly came about. The playwrights of the 1950s assailed us and then, for the most part, faded away; various firework novelists followed them in the 1960s and as rapidly fell as damp squibs; there followed the band wagon of *Oh! Calcutta* and its dubious brethren, led for the most part by persons with neither taste nor talent. The gutter took over; the stench was noisome. A new generation of writers sprang up with no other purpose than to tell all, revolting or revoltingly silly though it might be; public copulation, with all the attendant vocabulary, was abroad on stage and screen and no less palpably evident on the printed page. All these things were repeated in America, *ad nauseam*, too.

This, then, was the era of "tell all": the worst possible climate and conditions in which the short story could be expected to flourish. For in the short story, you cannot possibly tell all; this is the road to confusion and negation. In writing the short story, it is essentials that matter. As in a great drawing, so in a great short story: it is the lines that are left out that are of paramount importance. Not that this is all; it is knowing what lines to leave out that is of the greatest importance, too. There is in one of Tchehov's letters a reply of his to a correspondent who wished to have Tchehov's opinion on X, a minor Russian writer of the time. Tchehov's reply is illuminating in its brevity: "I long to rewrite it," he wrote, "*lacily*". Exactly. "Lacily" is the *mot juste*, expressing the very essence of what the short story should be, showing that it must depict more by implication than by statement, more by what is left out than left in. It ought, in fact, to resemble lace: strong but delicate, deviously woven yet full of light and air.

The antithesis of all this is the school of "tell all," which may otherwise be called "the school of stodge," the school where all is offered and nothing left to the imagination, the perception, or the wit of the reader. At the same time, largely due to the war, yet another phenomenon appeared: namely that of the so-called reportage, the factual, or documentary school of writing. The latter was the death-kiss also of many British films before, during, and after the war. An even more bastard form eventually raised its obtuse, ugly head: a creature known as documentary fiction. No such animal can of course exist, since the very definition is a contradiction in terms. What is fiction cannot be documentary, what is documentary cannot be fiction. The business of writing fiction is, in fact, an exercise in the art of telling lies. If the writer tells these lies with all the art and skill he is able to command then he will not only persuade his readers that what he is telling them is the truth but also that it is truer than life itself: all of which brings us back to Thackeray's well-known dictum that "the work of fiction contains more truth in solution than the work which purports to be all true." In other words it is through fidelity to imagination and not fidelity to observation that the truth will be revealed.

My prophecy as to the probability of a new golden age of the short story, such as we had on both sides of the Atlantic in the 1920s and 1930s was, therefore, dismally unfulfilled. There were of course other factors mitigating against it, not the least of them being the economic situation. Even before the war in England the little magazines to which writers of my generation contributed and were very glad to contribute, were already dead or dying. Nor was it merely little magazines that disappeared; in America even a magazine such as Colliers, with a reputed circulation of some millions, was unable to survive; other notable names followed it. Everywhere, therefore, the market for stories dwindled. Young writers, however

9

ardent their desire to write short stories and live by them, found themselves forced, by the sheer economics of the business, into spheres that offered security: novels, plays and some television drama. Nor could they be blamed for this.

This then is the situation of the short story today; if it is not quite one of unmitigated gloom it is certainly not bright. Nor can I myself see it, in a world of rising costs, not only of printing and production but in the very cost of living itself, getting any brighter. It is said that D. H. Lawrence, as a young man, managed on ten shillings a week; another short story writer friend of mine certainly lived on a pound; I, rather more fortunate, scraped along on two pounds. I do not need to point out the ludicrous nature of all this in relation to the literary world of today. Like Somerset Maugham and Joseph Conrad, who firmly rejected the idea of living in a garret, I have no use for starvation as a means of inspiring writers to create masterpieces. They are better done on full bellies.

To this pessimistic picture must be added the fact that the reading public, not only in Britain and America, but also on the continent, shows no disposition to revise its age-old prejudice against reading short stories in volume form. It grants some exceptions to this, of course, as in the case of Maugham, Kipling and some others, but by and large it views volumes of short stories with grave and unwarranted suspicion. The young short story writer, even if able to get his stories published between two covers, need look for no vast fortune in that direction.

Still, paradoxically, great numbers of people yearn to write short stories. A competition for short stories in a national newspaper some few years back is said to have produced the staggering figure of 50,000 entries, of which only the merest handful were publishable. I do not propose to examine here the causes of so lamentable a state of affairs. I will merely repeat what I have said time and time again: that the short story is the most difficult and exacting of all prose forms; it cannot be treated as a spare-time occupation; and above all it must not be allowed to foster the illusion, as I pointed out earlier in this preface, that its very brevity makes it easy to do.

All this brings me to a restatement of what *The Modern Short Story* purports to be and do. It does *not* exist as a manual of instruction for writing short stories; such was never my intention. It examines, instead, the work of many of the most distinguished masters of the form, confiding almost all of its investigations into the form as evolved in the 19th century and as we know it today: an essentially modern art.

Writing a short story may be compared with building a house with match-sticks. There comes a point in its construction when the addition of another stick may well bring down the whole affair in ruins. Thus balance is one of the supreme essentials to its creation and nowhere is this more true than in the very short story, say of one thousand words or less, or in the *novella*, fifteen or twenty times as long.

If it should be thought that one thousand words is really short then I recommend a glance at the Authorized Version of *The Prodigal Son*. This long-renowned and beautiful story contains something just over 130 words and begins with what would at first appear to be an extremely ordinary sentence: "A certain man had two sons". I suggest, on the contrary, that it is a very remarkable sentence, introducing as it does the story's three main characters in exactly six words. Here indeed is true economy.

Balance without stiffness, economy without cramp, essentials that are not merely bare bones, a canvas of scene and character which, though only a quarter or even a tenth of the size of the novel, must nevertheless satisfy the reader just as much and do so, as I have already remarked, perhaps more by what it leaves out than by what it puts in—these are merely a few of the technical challenges that make the *novella* so fascinating to the truly creative artist. It is moreover important not only that the reader should be satisfied but that, as at the end of a perfectly created meal, he should be left wanting a little more—or in other words that his curiosity and interest in the author's characters is still sharp enough to make him want to walk out with them beyond the printed page.

"Fiction," it has been said, "is the natural heir to poetry"; if this is true, and I firmly believe it is, I find it equally true that the short story is to fiction what the lyric is to poetry. In its finest mould the short story is, in fact, a prose poem. If the reader of *The Modern Short Story* absorbs this truth as he reads then the purpose of this book will have been fully justified.

H. E. BATES, 1971

THE MODERN SHORT STORY

CHAPTER I

RETROSPECT

THE history of the novel is short : covering only, if we
date its invention from Richardson, a period of two
hundred years. The history of the short story, through
its phases of myth and legend, fable and parable, anecdote
and pictorial essay, sketch, and even down to what the
crudest provincial reporter calls " a good story," cannot
be measured. The account in Genesis of the conflict
between Cain and Abel is a short story ; the parable of
the Prodigal Son is a short story, and in itself a masterpiece of compression for all time ; the stories of Salome,
Ruth, Judith, and Susannah are all examples of an art
that was already old, civilized, and highly developed
some thousands of years before the vogue of *Pamela.*
At what date, then, shall we begin an examination of its
history ? The paradoxical answer is that the history of
the short story, as we know it, is not vast but very brief.
" The short story proper," says Mr. A. J. J. Ratcliff,
" that is, a deliberately fashioned work of art, and not
just a straightforward tale of one or more events,

13

belongs to modern times " ; [1] " the short story is a young art," says Miss Elizabeth Bowen, " as we know it, it is a child of this century " ; [2] to this I shall only add an earlier judgment of my own that " the history of the English short story is very brief, for the simple reason that before the end of the nineteenth century it had no history." [3] It is therefore with this aspect of the short story, the development of the last hundred years—more pointedly still of the last forty or fifty years—that the present volume will deal.

It is clear, in that case, that there are many things with which it will not deal. Of two thousand years of story evolution only one-twentieth will be examined, and of that remaining twentieth only a part dissected. Dickens wrote short stories, but as far as the present survey goes he could well have saved his ink ; Defoe, Meredith, Thackeray, and many other English novelists of the eighteenth and nineteenth centuries also wrote short stories, but they recall too often the dish hashed up from the left-overs of the joint ; Henry James wrote short stories, but it is the influence rather than the achievement of his art that will be examined ; Kipling wrote short stories, but their value will seem of less account than that of comparatively little-known names such as A. E. Coppard, Katherine Mansfield, V. S. Pritchett, Dorothy Edwards, Katherine Ann Porter, Malachi

[1] A. J. J. Ratcliff : ed. *Short Stories by H. G. Wells* (2 volumes, Nelson)

[2] Elizabeth Bowen : *The Faber Book of Modern Stories* (Faber)

[3] H. E. Bates : " The Short Story " (*Lovat Dickson's Magazine* and *Story*, New York)

Whitaker, H. A. Manhood, Sean O'Faoláin, and others ; James Joyce wrote *Ulysses*, but here at any rate *Dubliners* will seem of greater importance ; Somerset Maugham will be accounted a better writer than Kipling, in some ways his nearest prototype, but a poorer writer than Joyce, whose impregnable reputation rests on one solitary, delicate, and long unwanted volume. O. Henry will be regarded just as one in the succession of those many American short story writers who created the most important indigenous tradition outside nineteenth-century Russia. And so on. Constantly throughout the survey of the modern story one is struck by the fact that the reputation is often of less importance than the art ; the unknown, unprofessional writer appears with a fine, even a great, story ; the voice speaks once and is silent ; but by this isolated achievement the frontiers of the short story may be pushed forward a significant fraction, and the flexibility of the art shown, once again, to be infinite.

The basis of almost every argument or conclusion I can make is the axiom that the short story can be anything the author decides it shall be ; it can be anything from the death of a horse to a young girl's first love affair, from the static sketch without plot to the swiftly moving machine of bold action and climax, from the prose poem, painted rather than written, to the piece of straight reportage in which style, colour, and elaboration have no place, from the piece which catches like a cobweb the light subtle iridescence of emotions that can never be really captured or measured to the solid tale in which all emotion, all action, all reaction is measured, fixed, puttied, glazed, and finished, like a well-built house, with three coats of shining and enduring paint. In that infinite flexibility, indeed, lies the reason why the short story has never been adequately defined.

Many definitions have been, and always are being, attempted. Wells defined the short story as any piece of short fiction that could be read in half an hour. Poe, sometimes acclaimed its modern originator, declared that " in the whole composition there should be no word written, of which the tendency, direct or indirect, is not to one pre-established design." Tchehov held that a story should have neither beginning nor end, but reminded authors that if they described a gun hanging on the wall on page one, sooner or later that gun must go off. Mr. John Hadfield describes the short story as " a story that is not long." [1] The late Sir Hugh Walpole, in a moment of truly remarkable perception, asserted that " a story should be a story : a record of things happening, full of incident and accident, swift movement, unexpected development, leading through suspense to a climax and a satisfying dénouement." [2] Jack London declared that it should be " concrete, to the point, with snap and go and life, crisp and crackling and interesting." Miss Elizabeth Bowen, rightly wary of the concrete definition, says, " the first necessity of the short story, at the set out, is *necessariness*. The story, that is to say, must spring from an impression or perception pressing enough,

[1] John Hadfield : ed. *Modern Short Stories* (Everyman)
[2] J. W. Marriott : ed. *A Modern Anthology of Short Stories* (Nelson)

acute enough, to have made the writer write." [1]   The
late E. J. O'Brien, to whom the short story in Britain
and America owes an unpayable debt, holds that " the
first test of a short story, in any qualitative analysis, is
the measure of how vitally compelling the writer makes
his selected facts or incidents." [2]   Mr. Ellery Sedgewick,
who pounced on the genius of Hemingway's *Fifty Grand*
when that story had been rejected by half the editors of
America, holds that " a story is like a horse race.   It is
the start and finish that count most." [3]   Finally, Mr. A. E.
Coppard bases the whole theory of his work on the
essential difference between a story, as something which
is written, and a tale, as something which is told.

All of these definitions have one thing in common.
None of them has a satisfactory finality ; none defines
the short story with an indisputable epigrammatic
accuracy which will fit all short stories.   For Tchehov,
the craftsman, beginning and end do not matter ; for
Mr. Sedgewick, the editor, beginning and end are everything.   Yet both are right.   Mr. Hadfield's definition will
fit a thousand stories yet fail to account satisfactorily for
Death in Venice, Family Happiness, or *The Gentleman from
San Francisco.*   Sir Hugh Walpole's definition will do
admirably for a work by O. Henry but fails miserably
on application to Tchehov's *The Darling,* Mrs. Malachi
Whitaker's *Frost in April,* or the unpredictable sketches

---

[1] Elizabeth Bowen : ed. *Faber Anthology of Modern Stories* (Faber)

[2] E. J. O'Brien : ed. *The Best Short Stories: 1918 et seq.* (Cape)

[3] Sedgewick and Dominovitch : ed. *Novel and Story* (Atlantic
Monthly Press)

of Mr. Saroyan. One does not measure the beauty of landscape with a tape measure. Jack London's demand for a concoction with " snap and go and life " is a perfect answer for those who like whisky, but it will be lost on those whose taste has been educated to the bouquet of Turgenev or James Joyce's *The Dead*. It is only when Mr. Ellery Sedgewick asserts, in his extremely perceptive essay written for American schools, " So it is that the short story has become all sorts of things, situation, episode, characterization, or narrative—in effect a vehicle for every man's talent," [1] that we come back again to the sensible conclusion that the short story, whether short or long, poetical or reported, plotted or sketched, concrete or cobweb, has an insistent and eternal fluidity that slips through the hands.

This is, and has always been, my own view. The impression that the short story has something of the indefinite and infinitely variable nature of a cloud is one which sooner or later must be forced on anyone who not only reads, but attempts to break down analytically, the work of writers differing so vastly as Turgenev and Hemingway, Sherwood Anderson and O. Henry, George Moore and Stephen Crane, Kipling and Katherine Mansfield. Is the cumulus or the cirrus more beautiful ? The thunder-cloud or the flotilla of feathers ? The calm blue and white of noon, or the savagery of sunset ? There is no definition, no measure, which will aptly contain the structure, effect, and beauty of them all. As

[1] Sedgewick and Dominovitch : ed. *Novel and Story* (Atlantic Monthly Press)

the sky is not made of bricks, so it is worth remembering that stories are not put together with plumb-line and trowel.

There is one other thing which these many and varied definitions all have in common. All omit to point out the advantages of elasticity, in both choice of character and use of time, which the short story holds over the novel. The novel is predominantly an exploration of life : reflecting and describing in some form the impact, entanglement, fruition, destruction or fulfilment of human emotions and desires. "Characters begin young; they grow old ; they move from scene to scene, from place to place," said Virginia Woolf.[1] This development of character, this forward movement of time, have always been and perhaps always will be the pulse and nerve of the novel. But in the short story time need not move, except by an infinitesimal fraction ; the characters themselves need not move ; they need not grow old ; indeed there may be no characters at all. A novel without characters would be a tiresome affair ; but a novel with characters who never spoke a word would surely be more tiresome still. Yet many a good short story has characters who never open their lips. A novel whose characters were never named, whose location and time were never stated, might well impose on its readers a strain that they would justifiably refuse to bear. Yet many a short story has characters which bear no more marks of identification than the

[1] Virginia Woolf : *The Leaning Tower* (Folios of New Writing, ed. John Lehmann, Hogarth Press)

anonymous and universal label of " boy " or " girl,"
" man " or " woman," " the traveller " or " the commercial traveller," " the barmaid " or " the soldier," and
no more topographical exactitude than "the street," " the
field," " the room," or any seashore between Brighton
and Botany Bay.

"The Novel," said Edward Garnett, " can be anything
according to the hands which use it " —a truth far
more widely applicable to the short story. For the short
story remains plastic, and continues to increase its plasticity, as long as human nature remains the infinitely
plastic and variable thing it is. In the 'nineties Kipling
was writing of India from a viewpoint that was so popular
and so widely endorsed that it might well have seemed,
to the Empire-drunken Britisher of the day, to give the
only right and proper view; in 1940 young native Indian
writers have something to say of their own country from
a viewpoint so unsuspected, so unheard of, and so real
that Kipling seems guilty of nothing but plain falsification. Again in the 'nineties, when O. Henry was perform-
ing elaborate conjuring tricks with an amazing collection
of comic human paraphernalia and the result was
accepted with the same universal applause as Kipling
had enjoyed, who could have guessed that fifty years
later a young American-Armenian named Saroyan
would demonstrate how a conjuring trick could be
performed without any human paraphernalia at all, but
with only a pair of eyes, a typewriter, and a hand-
kerchief to dry his tears ?

In its various stages of development the short story

has frequently been compared with some other literary form, sometimes with some artistic form outside literature. It is thus declared to have affinities with the drama ; with the narrative ballad ; with the lyric and the sonnet. In the last thirty years it has shown itself, as in fact much other writing has, to be pictorial rather than dramatic, to be more closely allied to painting and the cinema than to the stage. Mr. A. E. Coppard has long cherished the theory that short story and film are expressions of the same art, the art of telling a story by a series of subtly implied gestures, swift shots, moments of suggestion, an art in which elaboration and above all explanation are superfluous and tedious. Miss Elizabeth Bowen advances the same idea :

The short story . . . in its use of action is nearer to the drama than to the novel. The cinema, itself busy with a technique, is of the same generation : in the last thirty years the two arts have been accelerating together. They have affinities—neither is sponsored by a tradition ; both are, accordingly, free ; both, still, are self-conscious, show a self-imposed discipline and regard for form ; both have, to work on, immense matter—the disorientated romanticism of the age.[1]

This is strikingly true. Indeed the two arts have not only accelerated together but have, consciously or not, taught each other much. The scrap of dirty paper blown by wind along the empty morning street, a girl sewing,

[1] Elizabeth Bowen : *Faber Book of Modern Stories* (Faber)

on a railway station, the tear in her lover's jacket and he hiding it by holding up a suitcase, a mother staring dumbly at her returned gangster son — these tiny moments, seen as it were telescopically, brightly focused, unelaborated and unexplained, stamp swiftly on the mind the impressions of desolation, embarrassed love, or maternal despair. Each moment implies something it does not state ; each sends out a swift brief signal on a certain emotional wave-length, relying on the attuned mental apparatus of the audience to pick it up.

That audience, it seems to me, becomes of increasingly greater importance; but more important still, I feel, becomes the attitude of writer or director towards that audience. Are its powers of reception and perception to be consistently underestimated ? In a process of under-estimation what happens ? At the extreme a writer takes a character and describes not only his physique, his weight, his moustache and glasses, but also his clothes, his manner, and his mannerisms, his taste in food and drink, all in minute detail—in order to eliminate any possibility, it seems, of his being confused with the clothes-prop.

This, a century ago, and indeed with some writers for long afterwards, was the accepted convention. Dickens, artist though he was, played throughout novel after novel, with gusto and brilliance, this game of under-estimating the reader : so much so that he not only described every character by the system of catalogue but, in many cases, and because he was often writing a serial story that was to be read in parts, reissued that catalogue

22

after an interval in which he judged the reader might have forgotten what goods were for sale.

This was all very well, and in many cases delightful fun, in a novel of 200,000 words ; but to apply the same method to the short story was rather like dressing a six-months-old baby in a top-hat and fur coat, with the inevitable result—suffocation. Hence, I think, the languishing of the short story in England throughout the first three-quarters of the nineteenth century, when no single writer applied to it a technique different from that of the novel ; and its gradual emergence, accelerated during the last thirty years, as a separate form addressed to a reader who was presumed to be able to take many previously elaborated things such as physical descriptions for granted.

The evolution of the short story may therefore, I think, have something to do with the evolution of the general reader. We must be wary of condemning Dickens, when it would be more just, perhaps, to condemn an age more confined to compartments of class, place, and prejudice than our own. Dickens, often publishing a novel in monthly parts, found it necessary to devote some hundreds of words, and if necessary repeat those words a month later, to a single character. In 1920 Sherwood Anderson remarked simply that " she was a tall silent woman with a long nose and troubled grey eyes " ; in 1930 Mr. Ernest Hemingway in a moment, for him, of unusual expansion, said, " He wore a derby hat and a black overcoat buttoned across his chest. His face was small and white and he had tight

23

lips. He wore a silk muffler and gloves." In 1940 Mr. V. S. Pritchett writes, " He had a cape on, soaked with rain, and the rain was in beads in his hair. It was fair hair. It stood up on end."

Anderson took up fourteen words, Mr. Hemingway thirty-one, Mr. Pritchett twenty-six. Between Dickens and Mr. Pritchett, then, something has happened. Is it only the evolution of the short story ? May it not also be, perhaps, the parallel evolution of the reader ? Education, travel, wider social contact, the increased uniformity of life, dress, and manners have made us all familiar with things that were once remote enough to need to be described. To-day all of us have seen Sherwood Anderson's woman, the tragic, anonymous representative of a whole inarticulate class ; we have seen Mr. Hemingway's tough with the black overcoat and bowler hat ; we know Mr. Pritchett's type with its fair hair that stands up on end. The widening of social contact, among other things, has relieved these three writers, and their generation, of an oppressive obligation. It is no longer necessary to describe ; it is enough to suggest. The full-length portrait, in full dress, with scenic background, has become superfluous; now it is enough that we should know a woman by the shape of her hands.

In this way the short story can be seen not as a product evolved by generations of writers united in a revolutionary intention to get the short story more simply, more economically, and more truthfully written, but as something shaped also by readers, by social expansion, and by what Miss Bowen calls " peaks of common experience." For there has not been, and rarely is, any such united revolution among writers. Writers work, die, and leave legacies. Other writers draw on those inheritances, as Katherine Mansfield did on Tchehov's, and in turn leave others. But in their turn, too, readers live and perhaps succeed in raising, by an infinitely small fraction, the level of common experience and artistic receptivity. To that level the short story must adjust itself.

How it has gradually adjusted itself, expanding and yet rarefying its range, from Poe to Pritchett, Kipling to Coppard, is something that the succeeding chapters may possibly show.

Chapter II

ORIGINS : GOGOL AND POE

Nicolai Vasilievitch Gogol was born at Sorochintsky, in Russia, in 1809 ; in exactly the same year Edgar Allan Poe was born in Baltimore. Gogol was educated at Niezhin ; Poe at Stoke Newington in England. Gogol died in 1852, Poe in 1849. And from these two short lives may be said to flow the twin streams of the modern short story.

The phrase—I think it was Gorky's—"We all spring from Gogol's *Overcoat*," is one of wide truth ; for Gogol is something more than the father of the modern short story in all its manifestations of poetic realism, and of that excellent short story in particular, which in its pictorial accuracy and emotional liveliness seems to-day as modern as ever. Gogol marks the switch-over from romanticism to the thing which, for want of a better expression, we still call realism ; he marks the beginning of the wider application of visual writing, of vivid objectivity, of that particular faith in indigenous material which is to-day the strength of the American short story, and the absence of which brought it to such puerile levels thirty years ago. Gogol is the father of all writers who say, "I believe the lives of ordinary human folk,

26

rich or poor, adventurous or parochial, good or depraved, dull or exciting, constitute the only vein of
material a writer need ever seek or work." Gogol, like
all good writers since, looked outside his back door—
initially that of his mother's farm at Dikanka—and saw
a life that clashed within itself with such remarkably
diverse virility that there was no need to look farther.
That act of Gogol's was of extreme importance to the
short story : for until someone did that, the short story
as we know it to-day had no existence. As long as prose
writing remained flowery, turning on elegant periods,
and as long as the vision of the eye behind it remained
fogged by romantic conceptions and romantic social
prejudices and conventions—it was not many years
since only kings and gentlemen were heroes—then the
short story had little chance of renaissance. For the
structure of the short story is too delicate, too tenuous,
for a load of verbal pomposity. Load it with opinions,
observations, moral attitudes, stage embroidery, and it
breaks down, just as surely as the novel, in Victorian
times at any rate, became by these same things held up.
But as the father of the short story Gogol, it seems to me,
did a very simple thing, for which countless writers of
stories are indebted to him and the results of which may
be directly seen in the work of such writers as Coppard,
O'Flaherty, Joyce, Sherwood Anderson, Saroyan, and
many others to-day. He took the short story some way
back to the folk-tale, and in doing so bound it to
earth.

But it is obvious that Gogol's nationalism, in which he

was incidentally inspired by Pushkin, his lyricism, his realism, and his touch of folk exuberance, are not the whole of the short story, and while Gogol was eagerly writing to his mother for any detail of peasant life and custom that would confirm or amplify his childhood impressions of the fertile Ukraine, something else was happening in Boston and Baltimore. Poe was embarking on that series of nightmare excursions, touched by a sort of wild poetry, which earned him too the title of " father of the short story," and whose influence was subsequently to be every bit as wide as that of Gogol. The commonly quoted opinion that Poe was, and up to the close of the nineteenth century remained, a vastly fertile influence on the short story, is not one with which I should quarrel ; but when I read that " he brought the short story to a point of technical perfection which has never been surpassed," [1] then I can only think that in an examination of Poe's work a sense of balance is a sorely needed quality. Poe indeed belongs to that class of ripe-flavoured writers the flavour of whose work arises not so much from technical perfection as from some inner and indefinable quality that in turn arises from the man. That quality is sometimes, as in D. H. Lawrence, almost physical ; sometimes, as in Turgenev, a kind of fragrance; sometimes, as in Maupassant, a sort of calculating provincial shrewdness. It is these indefinite but powerful qualities, which are the man behind the writer, that are incapable of transmission from one artist to another. They are the dog beneath the skin : forces

[1] Clark and Lieber : *Great Short Stories of the World* (Heinemann)

quite apart from something technical, forces that are in reality the blood-stream of the work.

Of this kind of writer Poe was a remarkable example. Throughout his stories runs this intransmissible something. It is clearly the result of a deep complex psychical state ; Poe, like Lawrence, was a sick man ; so that the subsequent effect, in story after story, is that of high emotional and nervous tension. The pages are darkly dyed with morbidity ; the echoes are those of souls beating their hands on the walls of mad-houses. "True ! nervous, very, very dreadfully nervous I had been and am ; but why *will* you say that I am mad ? " —the voice is that of the narrator in *The Tell-Tale Heart*, but it might equally be the voice of Poe. This powerful emotional state, producing in turn an atmosphere of terror, madness, half-madness, horror, suspense, and fear, is the thing for which Poe is famous. As a craftsman, and sometimes he is very good indeed, all his efforts are second to and governed by the peculiar power of his own emotional state. For this reason Poe, though he became a wide influence, imparted his greatest influence not to the short story in general but to a particular branch of it : the branch of detection and the uncanny.

Poe, who in turn was influenced by the fantasies of the German Hoffmann, is thus master of only certain branches of an art that is capable of putting forth an indefinite number of branches. Moreover, the nineteenth century was ripe for Poe. The new era of scientific discovery, the amazing interest in spiritualism—it claimed to have

1,500,000 adherents in America alone exactly ten years after Poe's death — the vast forces of age-old superstition set grumbling by the touch of education, a public inexhaustibly hungry for melodrama and the supernatural, a sudden increase in those who could read and could now enact for themselves the flesh-creeps of the ghost story in the glimmer of the rush-light—all these things, not forgetting the melodramatic spread of a religion that captured and held its adherents by fear and the exploitation of both the glamour and the terror of the unknown, made the age completely ready for the spread of Poe's particular virus. Poe is therefore really a little writer (as compared with Tolstoy, Hardy, Defoe, Dostoevsky, or Dickens) who was magnified to the size of a big writer by the almost supernatural fortune of being born at the right moment in the right country. Just as Shaw at the end of the century skilfully anticipated and exploited the forces that were rising against social injustice, religious superstition, and muddled thinking about the cosmos and the cash, so Poe, with a kind of clairvoyance, anticipated the vast nineteenth-century hunger for dream-worlds, scientific fantasy, and the mystery-drama of the dividing line between known and unknown.

One other thing, it seems to me, contributed to Poe's success. He was the first man of undoubted talent and distinguished force of temperament, outside Europe at any rate, to accept the story as a distinctive form at a moment when it was in no competitive danger from any other prose form. The Elizabethan short story had failed to survive the overwhelming counter-popularity of the drama and its greatest exponent, partly because it had no writers of comparable genius, partly because the story seen on the stage was far more exciting than the story read at home (even if you could read it), and partly because writers such as Greene and Nash seem to have had little conscious idea of how to relate a prose tale. As it was then eclipsed by the drama, the short story was later eclipsed, in the eighteenth century, by the rise of the novel, the heroic couplet, and the tittle-tattle essay. Its every chance of revival was frustrated by the advent of some other new or revitalized form for which the age was more ready or the public showed a preference.

Poe suffered from no such handicap. The drama offered no opposition. The novel was certainly about to be launched on a century of popular splendour, but the two arts were never rivals, and towards the end of that century, often to the detriment of the story, they were to develop side by side. Poe, like those following him, was fortunate in another respect. An element called the Public was to become an increasingly powerful force in every civilized country, so that where one person had read Greene, one thousand, more likely ten thousand, could now read Poe. Still another element, the magazine, was to give Poe and all his nineteenth- and twentieth-century successors a platform that extended round the world. Without that platform the short story could never, I think, have been what it is to-day.

Though Poe is important for himself, therefore, it seems to me that he is still more important as an example of a sublime coincidence of forces : the forces of his own genius, of a new era, of the hunger of a vast, new, illimitable public. Yet if I were asked to decide whether Gogol was not only a better writer but an infinitely more important influence on the development of the story, I should say yes. At the same time I could not name, I think, a handful of writers who bear on their work the Gogol imprint, even though we are all descended from *The Overcoat*, whereas I could name scores upon scores of writers marked with the definite and indelible imprint of Poe.

Poe's main influences are three, and they have been admirably put by Mr. A. J. J. Ratcliff[1] in some brief remarks on the story's development as a form :

> He excelled in the study of passive horror (*The Pit and the Pendulum*, about the Spanish Inquisition), the murder mystery (*The Murders in the Rue Morgue*) in which he preceded Gaboriau and Conan Doyle, and scientific puzzles and thrills (*The Gold Bug*) in which he gave a lead to H. G. Wells. In his tales the atmosphere is morbid and scaring, and is largely dependent on a hypnotically musical latinized style. His construction is masterly, indeed mathematically exact.

This short statement contains the key-words to Poe's genius : atmosphere, hypnotics, mathematical exactitude. Of these it is interesting to note that at least two, the first and the last, are qualities of whose essential

[1] A. J. J. Ratcliff: ed. *Short Stories by H. G. Wells* (2 volumes, Nelson)

importance nearly every short story writer of quality has given proof. Even Tchehov, carelessly regarded by popular opinion as an essayist revealing character through a series of casual and insignificant incidents, is in reality a master of precision. Atmosphere and precision, however subtly concealed, are in fact two of the cardinal points in the art of the short-story writer, and it is notable that both are among the strongest characteristics of Poe.

So Poe's influence, though it touches only three particular branches of the story, is academically sound. Poe understood to perfection the art, as I believe Tennyson put it, "of wrapping it up so that the fools don't know it." His most famous successors, notably Wells and Conan Doyle, understood it too.

Nevertheless something happened to the short story, after Poe had finished with it, that even he, with all his psychic imagination, could probably never have foreseen. The defect of one man is often the strong point of another. Poe's defect was that he was not interested in the ordinary ; his joy was in the extraordinary. I doubt therefore if he could have guessed that a century after his death the short story would be in the hands of writers whose whole art was concentrated on an interpretation of ordinary, as opposed to fancified, human beings.

This tremendous change—and it can be seen that even the detective-mystery story eventually reached a stage when the very authenticity of its horrors depended on the realism with which its everyday backgrounds and

33

characters were painted, as can plainly be observed in Doyle—could not possibly have come about if Poe had really " brought the short story to a point of technical perfection which has never been surpassed."

Like most developments in art, the nineteenth-century development of the short story was the result not of a single influence but of the clash of several influences. Music, painting, and writing are fortunately exportable commodities which in time reach and influence artists far from their country of origin. So with Poe, whose influence met that of Gogol, Tolstoy, Turgenev, and Flaubert not in the streets of Baltimore but on the banks of the Seine. The French, interested always in precise forms of any art, naturally welcomed a new development of the short story. Balzac, Mérimée, and Gautier are all roughly contemporary with Poe, but it was not until the influence of Tolstoy, Turgenev, and Flaubert began to be felt in the salons of Paris that the short story was to move forward, revitalized, towards the form in which by the end of the century it became internationally famous and popular.

It is therefore not quite true to say, as has often been said, that the short story spread from the United States to France. Balzac in the eighteen-thirties was writing stories prodigiously ; and by 1846, that is before Poe had died, Turgenev had produced a series of what are, in spite of all their poetry, terrible pictures of the conditions of Russian serfdom—the stories which we know in English as *The Sportsman's Sketches*. That volume alone, with its poetry, its sensuous reaction to natural

34

beauty, its passionate nationalism and its sympathy with the underdog, was a landmark in the progress of the short story comparable only in importance to the publication of *Boule de Suif*, the Tchehov stories, Sherwood Anderson's *Winesburg Ohio*, and the stories of Mansfield and Hemingway. Its influence, delayed for fifty years through a series of execrable translations, was ultimately to spread to inestimable and rather surprising distances in England. Conrad, Galsworthy, George Moore, and, among living writers, Mr. Sean O'Faoláin, are only a few to whom *The Sportsman's Sketches* constitute a formative influence far more important than Poe ; even the materialistic Arnold Bennett confessed that Turgenev had influenced him as much as any other writer ; nor would it surprise me if one day Mr. Ernest Hemingway, the sap of whose work runs very softly under the outer skin of toughness, should make precisely the same confession.

Thus both the eastern and western developments of the short story were meeting in France, with what rich and in turn highly influential results we shall see later. But meanwhile what of our own country ? Taking the date as 1850, who was writing ? Scott was dead ; Dickens, Thackeray, Meredith, George Eliot, Charlotte Brontë, Mrs. Gaskell, and Trollope were all alive : an impressive if at times rather suety list of novelists. France had Balzac, America had Poe, Russia had Gogol, Turgenev, and, as it were, waiting in the wings, Tolstoy and Dostoevsky. All were writers of short stories : great stories, moreover, that were recognizably an expression of a separate form and not merely a *précis* of the novel. But if we search the English literary horizons of 1850 we search in vain for a short-story writer of the stature of Poe, Turgenev, or Kipling. Across that horizon goes one rather lonely and parochial figure, most famous now for a lavender-tinted miniature, whose American counterpart, Sarah Orne Jewett, was just opening childish eyes on the beloved landscape of New England. In that rather self-effacing figure, Elizabeth Cleghorn Gaskell, who to-day might have been a chronicler of the South Riding far more acute than the late Winifred Holtby, we see the only potentially important English short-story writer fade into the rather ponderous literary distances of the day.

The plain fact is that although we were to possess any number of novelists who occasionally cut out a short story from a scrap of material left over in the workroom, but were otherwise not interested in the separate form, we were to possess no short-story writer of real consequence for the next forty years, and not one who made a world reputation purely as a short-story writer until Kipling arrived. This is a staggering fact when we remember what Maupassant and Flaubert were doing in France, Tolstoy (the superb *Death of Ivan Ilytch* and *Family Happiness* are alone worth half the three-deckers of Victorian England) in Russia, and Bret Harte, Bierce, Sarah Orne Jewett, and even O. Henry and Jack London, in America. It is worth noting, too, that Tchehov, whose influence on the most modern development of the short story is still potent, was born in 1850.

For this extraordinary phase of arrested development there must be a reason, it seems to me, other than the simple fact that the novel was highly popular. The novel was also highly popular in France, Russia, and America, yet its popularity did not effect there a total suppression of the short story. The reason, I think, is twofold ; for there are two things the short story cannot carry, or two related conditions under which it cannot thrive. It cannot tolerate a weight of words or a weight of moral teaching, and it is highly significant that these two factors are dominant characteristics of the Victorian English novel. The heavily latinized, abstract prose style, with its Gothic-revival architecture, seen in all its impossibly affected perfection in Hardy and Meredith, is a weight under which the short story simply cannot breathe. Though it would be a mistake to suppose that the short story can tolerate nothing but a skin-bare simplicity of style, without a ray of elaboration or metaphor, it is certain that no short story could survive the sheer word-weight of the following passage :

Occasionally she came to a spot where independent worlds of ephemerons were passing their time in mad carousal, some in the air, some in the hot ground and vegetation, some in the tepid and stringy water of a nearly dried pool. All the shallower ponds had decreased to a vaporous mud amid which the maggoty shapes of innumerable obscene creatures could be indistinctly seen, heaving and wallowing with enjoyment. Being not a woman to philosophize she sometimes sat down under her umbrella to rest and watch their happiness, for a certain hopefulness as to the result of her visit gave ease to her mind, and between important thoughts left her free to dwell on any infinitesimal matter which caught her eyes.[1]

It will be argued, quite justly, that such a quotation as this, taken from a novel, does not fairly represent the craft exhibited by Hardy in the shorter form. It is true that Hardy, in his stories, shows occasional signs of recognizing that the short story demands a method more terse and direct than that of the novel. But the familiar woodenness remains ; the formal, substitute words are still too often not those of life, but literature :

As the sun passed the meridian and declined westward, the tall shadows from the scaffolding of Barnet's rising residence streaked the ground as far as to the middle of the highway.[2]

No schoolboy, to-day, would get marks for saying "passed the meridian and declined westward" when what he meant was "began to set" ; or for using "residence" instead of "house," "highway" instead of "road." Hardy is bound by a convention. Yet you see him now and then struggle out of it, in an admirable effort :

She was kneeling down in the chimney corner before two pieces of turf laid together with the

[1] Thomas Hardy : *The Return of the Native* (**Macmillan**)
[2] *Wessex Tales*

heather inwards, blowing at the red-hot ashes with her breath till the turves flamed.[1]

This is so good, pictorially, that one can only conclude that Hardy did not know it; for soon the convention has him back again:

He hardly saw that the dewy time of day lent an unusual freshness to the bushes and trees which had so recently put on their summer habit of heavy leafage.[2]

In short, the Hardy of the novels is also the Hardy of the short stories: the same curious mixture of earthiness and bookishness, of pomposity and simplicity; a man who does not recognize that the convention producing "their summer habit" of heavy leafage is a bad convention, or that the description of the girl blowing at the flaming turves is good. Again and again you get the impression, as in the novels, that there is a certain literary rate of progress that must be set and kept up; there is plenty of time, for both reader and writer, for explanations, reflections, formal descriptions. You get the impression, too, that Hardy is the local reporter turned literary man, who thinks the occasional exhibition of a little literary phraseology will give him dignity. Hardy lived in a period more dominated by the Church than ours, and sometimes you get also the impression of being sermonized. The language turns ecclesiastical:

[1] *Wessex Tales*
[2] *Ibid.*

The weight is gone from our lives; the shadow no longer divides us: then let us be joyful together as we are, dearest Vic, in the days of our vanity.

Do women ever speak to men like that? Was there ever a time when they spoke to them like that? The man who evidently thought they did hardly has a claim to be called a realistic writer. Yet Hardy's stories, perhaps even more than his novels, are bound by that impossible convention, and he evidently never understood that the short story cannot survive under these wooden words, or under the wooden explanations and wooden plots of which volumes like *A Changed Man* and *Wessex Tales* are full.

Contrast the above passages from Hardy's tales with a brief quotation from Turgenev:

The sky is a peacefully untroubled white through the bare brown branches; in parts, on the limes, hang the last golden leaves. The damp earth is elastic under your feet; the high dry blades of grass do not stir; long threads lie shining on the blanched turf, white with dew.[1]

This passage is not only of remarkable beauty; it has ceased, in Turgenev's hands, to be the ordinary "description of nature." It has a quality of porousness; it has absorbed the colour, fragrance, and hushed tranquillity

[1] Turgenev: *The Sportsman's Sketches*, trans. Constance Garnett (Heinemann)

of an autumn day ; so that at last it no longer indicates, but *is* the thing itself.

In such tender and skilful hands the short story thrives ; in hands such as Hardy's it is choked crudely to death, like a baby fed on a diet of two-inch steaks and porter.

Here, then, is an indication of the structural difficulties, of which I hope to say more later, under which the nineteenth-century English short story struggled to live. There remains the moral attitude ; that suffocating stranglehold which Butler threw off by *The Way of All Flesh*, the attitude in which " men have been known to think that poetry itself would be much more satisfactory if only it proved something, and even poets have been known to give them some excuse by professing to ' justify ' something to something else. . . . Milton himself was influenced by it. Wordsworth ruined much of his work by his determination to be a teacher." [1]

The notion that literature, and the novel especially, should teach something, that it should carry a lesson, a moral, or a message, and that its results should not give purely aesthetic, sensuous, and recreative pleasure, is one that dies very hard. This notion almost invariably springs from and is fostered by the public and not by writers, who nevertheless in Victorian times often succumbed to the weight of public demand. It seems ludicrous now to think that in its serial form (to be read by the sacred fireside) the passages in *Tess* where Angel Clare *carried* the girls across the stream had to be altered so that these girls were decently wheeled across in a

[1] H. S. Milford : intro. *English Short Stories*, Vol. I. (World's Classics)

wheelbarrow. Wherever parochial standards of taste and morality are allowed to influence or hamper the writer, the result can only be a loss to himself and to literature in his own day, and in some future day, when standards of taste and morality have changed, the cause of amazement and ridicule. So it seems incredible and ludicrous to us that *Tess* should have been banned, and *Jude* burned, when to-day their actions, which once brought the thunder from pulpits, seem only mistakes of timid triviality. The lesson there is clear for all writers : that they should never, from first to last, pay the least attention to public opinion, or to what is worse—public taste.

It was against the kind of public opinion and public taste that could not bear to read of young girls being carried across streams by young men that the nineteenth-century English short story had to struggle for life. Small wonder that it remained orphan, puny, and of little account. Yet this was not all. Throughout this era of what Virginia Woolf called " The Steady Tower,"[1] the English writer was earnestly engaged in romanticizing the life he saw. From Dickens alone do we seem to get the impression of a writer looking at everyday life in an attempt to paint it. But from the rest ? Virginia Woolf said :

> To the nineteenth-century writer human life must have looked like a landscape cut up into separate fields. In each was gathered a different group of people.

[1] Virginia Woolf : *The Leaning Tower* (Folios of New Writing, Autumn 1940)

Each to some extent had its own traditions ; its own manners ; its own speech ; its own dress ; its own occupation. . . . And the nineteenth-century writer did not seek to change those divisions ; he accepted them. He accepted them so completely that he became unconscious of them.

Here, then, is another laborious burden under which not only the short story, but all writing, laboured. Throughout the century great things were happening : social forces were being liberated ; wars were being fought ; empires carved out ; at the beginning of the century there had been widespread riots in rural districts, and soon after Victoria's accession almost a revolution. Do the writers of the time leave a picture of these things ? offer a comment on them ? The answer is almost invariably, except in the case of Dickens, Kingsley, Charlotte Brontë, or Reade, no. It is easy to see, partly at any rate, why this was so. News of wars, far empires, and pioneers, for example, travelled more slowly, much more slowly, than to-day, when it travels so fast that we even attempt to anticipate it and play at prophets. Now, too, war is of us, about us, on top of us ; no use hiding any more. The guns might thunder over the stench and gangrene and typhoid of the Crimea, but sound and stench and fury might all die away before ever they reached the ears of the writer of the day ; to-day the guns thunder over every man's roof and the bomb falls in every back garden. The writer is no longer the literary man, a person apart and aloof, stepping aside on the grass verge of life, book in hand, eyes on the sky, while the traffic of humanity streams past him. He is one with all the rest : the common man, perhaps the common fool, the brave, bewildered, victimized common denominator.

Whatever else posterity may say about the literature of the last fifty years, it will never be able to say, I think, that it did not leave a picture of its time, and in turn some sort of comment, vastly increased this last few years, on that picture. From Bennett and Wells down to modern regional writers like Mrs. Malachi Whitaker and Mr. Leslie Halward (in America their counterparts are numbered by hundreds) we can see a more and more conscientious tendency among writers to set down an objective impression of life as they see it and know it best. And here it may be worth remembering that both Bennett and Wells acknowledged a common master in Dickens, and a private master respectively in Turgenev and Poe.

So the conditions under which the short story could begin to thrive best, free from the poking of moral umbrellas, pseudo-Gothic prose, and class-bound writers, did not begin to exist in England until the 'nineties. Yet fifty years before that time Turgenev had done the very thing which no English writer had seemed capable ever of doing. He had stepped out of his class, the high Russian aristocratic, and had painted with tenderness, sympathy, accuracy, with purest colouring and the deepest poetic insight, the Russian serf and the Russian countryside. Tolstoy, another aristocrat, was to follow his example. Even in America Bret Harte (born in 1839) was to bring a touch of poetic realism to his excellent stories of the west. No one in England for many years was to do anything at all comparable with the short story : to train on it a vision at once sharp, poetical, imaginative, realistic, and unrestricted by the blinkers of class. Even when a short-story writer of some stature, Rudyard Kipling, arrived at last, his whole work was to be coloured by a rabid imperialism, the unfurling of class banners, and the mediocre heroics of his time.

CHAPTER III

AMERICAN WRITERS AFTER POE

My first acquaintance with the English short story was made when, as a boy of seventeen, I bought out of my pocket-money the two volumes of *Selected English Short Stories* (Series I. and II.), to which has since been added Series III., published in the World's Classics with an introduction by Dr. Hugh Walker. It was perhaps natural at the time that I did not read that introduction, afterwards found to be an extremely able piece of work, and it was equally natural that I did not notice for some years that more than one-third of the stories in Series I., and exactly one-half of the stories in Series II., were not by English writers at all, but by American.

It was this discovery that first gave me a clue to the poverty of the short story in nineteenth-century England, and an abiding respect for the short story in America. It is unthinkable that an anthologist of English poetry, drama, essay, or novel should ever be forced to borrow one-third or one-half of his material from another English-speaking country. If an established culture cannot provide representative examples of some particular form of art, the conclusion is that that branch of art is in an exceedingly bad way. If there had been decently representative English stories to choose, the editor of the World's Classics volumes would no doubt have chosen them. But those stories obviously did not exist : whereas in America, very luckily, they did.

The English nineteenth-century short story, up to the fertile period of the final years, offers no kind of continuity, no heritage passed on from writer to writer, on which either future historian or commentator can seize. Inspirational writers did not exist ; nor derivative. Wherever a writer of forceful quality or influential voice springs up, the derivative writer follows in his hundreds. Soon after Ernest Hemingway published *Men Without Women* and *A Farewell to Arms*, for example, the imitators of Hemingway's particular manner sprang up in every little town from Los Angeles to Long Island. Yet Hemingway, after the settling of years, begins to look quite traditional—as in fact he is : a descendant in a tradition which for a hundred years has been a distinctive, perhaps the most distinctive, part of American literature.

After Poe there is scarcely a decade of that literature that does not offer a short-story writer of interest or quality ; and at least two writers of stories, Irving and Hawthorne, both famous, were born before Poe. After Poe (1809), the ten-year recurrence of names is almost monotonous : Herman Melville (1819), Fitz-James O'Brien (1828), Bret Harte (1839), Ambrose Bierce (1842), Sarah Orne Jewett (1849), Mary E. Wilkins (1862), O. Henry (1867), Jack London (1876), Stephen

Crane (1871), and so on. These writers together form a lineage on which it is possible to work ; they inherit something from one another and push the story on through fresh phases of live development. What caused them to spring up and flourish and give distinction to a period that in England can show scarcely a single name of parallel importance at all ?

The answer is generally given that America, unhampered by tradition and class-barriers, was in a happier position to foster the story, which above all demanded speed and simplicity. Already its people were talking faster, moving faster, and apparently thinking faster : so it appeared likely that they might wish their writers to be writing faster. There is some truth in this, for it is worth noting that during the period when American literature showed its closest alignment with European models and methods, namely, the years immediately before, during, and after the first Great War, the American short story dropped to its lowest standard. Mr. John Cournos writes, " It has been vaguely asserted that the American temperament, evolved out of a preoccupation with concrete, practical matters, and a tendency to rush and hurry, demands its literature terse and to the point." The words " vaguely asserted " are correct ; for in both Canada and Australia new peoples were similarly preoccupied with " concrete, practical matters, and a tendency to rush and hurry " and were also in a position to demand a " literature terse and to

[1] John Cournos : intro. *American Short Stories of the Nineteenth Century* (Everyman's Library)

the point." Yet that literature, if ever they did demand it, was not forthcoming, and has not been forthcoming since.

Again, the American short story, though certainly free from restrictions of class and tradition, had to face a condition that operated just as powerfully as in England. Its horizons were darkened by the parochial umbrella, held grimly over creative art with puritanical obstinacy. How did it survive ? It was Bret Harte's own opinion that it survived through humour :

> It was *humour*, of a quality as distinct and original as the country and civilization in which it was developed. It was at first noticeable in the anecdote or " story," and, after the fashion of such beginnings, was orally transmitted. . . . Crude at first, it received a literary polish in the press, but its dominant quality remained. It was concise and condensed, yet suggestive. It was delightfully extravagant, or a miracle of understatement. . . . It gave a new interest to slang. . . . It was the parent of the American short story."

Time proves Bret Harte to have been right, I think for that same humour, reiterated with that same concise and suggestive understatement, is still the nerve of the American short story to-day. Humour is not essentially something allied with the comic ; it represents also an ability to obtain, and retain, a rigid sense of perspective. Without that faculty the vision of the short story has the woolliness of a lens improperly adjusted. A novel can survive such a condition for many pages—a reader may skim the results ; but those few pages *are* the short story, which, if improperly focused, can never survive. It is a certain quality of humour—seen admirably in Tchehov—that imposes a corrective on the writer's line of sight ; and it is that same quality, an instinct of balance rather than the working of conscious intelligence, that will save the short-story writer from redundancy, from the cardinal sin of saying too much.

Shaped by this native humour, the nineteenth-century American short story went some way back, like Gogol's stories of the Ukraine, to the folk-tale. It remained largely untouched by poetic feeling as refined in delicacy as that of Turgenev ; it never had the literary greatness and universality of Tolstoy. But it was very much alive. Its character, beauty, and fibre were like that of country-made furniture : conceived for utility, it took on beauty and style as a kind of happy accident. These character-istics became a natural integral part of the work, and remain so to-day.

It is significant that very many modern American short-story writers of reputation have been at some time or other journalists. Bret Harte was no exception. Work-ing first as schoolmaster, miner, and compositor, at the age of eighteen he joined a San Francisco paper, and to that paper contributed some of his first stories. Was it *The Atlantic Monthly* that later offered him thirty thousand dollars, or some such figure, to write for it ? The answer does not really matter. In a few years, with such stories as *Miggles, The Outcasts of Poker Flat, The Luck of Roaring Camp*, and *Tennessee's Partner*, Bret Harte had become something of a national institution. *The Luck of Roaring Camp*, was, in fact, a national sensation, and by means of it Bret Harte tapped a national demand. Like a good journalist Bret Harte knew the formula : people, humour, movement, colour, suspense, surprise, the touch of sentimentalism, the wave of regret, the laughter behind the tears. Unlike Stephen Crane, who later stepped into the scene with a method so naturally perfect that he never knew quite how good it was, Bret Harte was an accomplished showman who knew to perfection the art of dressing the shop window. He knew that the world loves nothing so much as elaboration of the theme of " behind that rough exterior there beats a heart of gold," or of the tender union of sworn enemies in the moment of death, the tear running down the hard and hoary cheek, or of " the Christmas dawn came slowly after." In his treatment of all these and similar themes there is a heap of nonsense ; but it is not the nonsense of pretentiousness, of the " artistic attitude." From the arresting beginning (" Sandy was very drunk ") to the fade-out (" and behind them the school of Red Mountain closed upon them for ever "), at which he was so accomplished, Bret Harte must have known that he was dressing up and giving an entertainment. He was an honest, if limited and second-rate, artist who to-day would have been a gold-mine in Hollywood, which recognizes and uses the same machinery of appeal : the ultimate triumph of good over evil, the heart of gold behind the rough exterior, the "hold me up, pal" scene of death, the tough-*hombre*-sweet-schoolmarm love affair, the laughter behind tears, the fade-out, the restful illusion of tranquillity after tribulation.

In 1860 Bret Harte was a national sensation; to-day he falls quietly into place among the second-rate, to be seen in the correct perspective of almost three-quarters of a century. For Bret Harte is really almost as significant for what he was not, as for what he was. The short story as conceived and marketed by Bret Harte offers no social comment, let alone a social criticism; it shows no sign that its author was moved to compassion, anger, or bitterness by the condition of the poor or by the wretched paradox of humanity in general. It has nothing to offer in the way of passionate nationalism or, as in Kipling, of rabid patriotism. Science, the machine, war, social problems or social bitterness might, for all Bret Harte cared, never have existed. Not that these things are essential to the short story, or to any writing at all; but it is interesting to note how far the short story, even in American hands, had still to go: and still more interesting to note that in its various phases and lapses of development it had still to go back and learn a lesson from Bret Harte—the lesson of regionalism, enforced by Sherwood Anderson, the lesson of learning to interpret its own people.

Of far greater significance than Bret Harte, a better writer, speaking from an intensely personal attitude, offering moreover a picture and some comment on the shattering history of his time, is the mysterious Ambrose

Bierce. Bierce served as an officer in the Civil War. A whole literature, dressed up, fattened out, romanticized, has now sprung up about that war in very much the same way as a whole literature sprang up in the nineteenth century about the Napoleonic Wars. It is comparatively easy now to sit back and, getting the perspective right, produce a *Gone With the Wind*. It is a very different matter to record the battle before the smoke has died away. In some dozens of forceful unromanticized war-sketches Bierce did that, and more. Bierce introduced the psychological study : perhaps more truthfully the pathological study. That he failed to raise it to the level where the pathological interest ceased to be obtrusive, to be sufficiently absorbed, does not really matter. Bierce is important as a sign of the days to come : the days when the short story was to interpret character not through a series of bold and attractive actions but through casual and apparently irrelevant incidents. As a man of action who in the stink of battle could retain a detached viewpoint Bierce was remarkable enough, and the famous *The Horseman in the Sky* alone would put him into the front rank of all commentators on the futility of war ; but as a man of action who was interested in the psychological value of the apparently insignificant moment or event Bierce was some years ahead of his time. It is interesting that he showed an inclination to keep the stories of action and the stories of interpretation separate, as if his two methods were imperfectly correlated. In Bierce, as in all writers of more than topical importance, and certainly not as in Bret Harte, two forces were in incessant conflict : spirit against flesh, normal against abnormal. This clash, vibrating in his work from beginning to end, keeping the slightest story nervous, restless, inquisitive, put Bierce into the company of writers who are never, up to the last breath, satisfied, who are never tired of evolving and solving some new equation of human values, who are driven and even tortured by their own inability to reach a conclusion about life and thereafter remain serene.

But Bierce, who as a writer tirelessly impinging a highly complex personality on every page will always remain interesting, is significant in another respect. Bierce began to shorten the short story ; he began to bring to it a sharper, more compressed method : the touch of impressionism.

> The snow had piled itself, in the open spaces along the bottom of the gulch, into long ridges that seemed to heave, and into hills that appeared to toss and scatter spray. The spray was sunlight, twice reflected ; dashed once from the moon, twice from the snow.

The language has a sure, terse, bright finality. In its direct focusing of the objects, its absence of woolliness and laboured preliminaries, it is a language much nearer to the prose of our own day than that of Bierce's day.

Again the same " modern " quality is found :

> A man stood upon a railroad bridge in northern Alabama, looking down into the swift water twenty

feet below. The man's hands were behind his back. his wrists bound with a cord. A rope closely encircled his neck.

Note that this is the beginning of a story, the famous *An Occurrence at Owl Creek Bridge*. Note that there is no leading-up, no preliminary preparation of the ground. In less than forty words, before the mind has had time to check its position, we are in the middle of an incredible and arresting situation. Writers throughout the ages have worked with various methods to get the reader into a tractable and sympathetic state of mind, using everything from the bribery of romanticism and fantasy to the short bludgeon blow of stark reality. But Bierce succeeds by a process of absurd simplicity : by placing the most natural words in the most natural order, and there leaving them. Such brief and admirable lucidity, expressed in simple yet not at all superficial terms, was bound to shorten the short story and to charge it in turn with a new vigour and reality. Not that Bierce always uses these same simple and forceful methods. Sometimes the prose lapses into the heavier explanatory periods of the time, and unlike the passages quoted, is at once dated ; but again and again Bierce can be found using that simple, direct, factual method of description, the natural recording of events, objects, and scenes, that we in our day were to know as reportage.

Born too early, working outside the contemporary bounds, Bierce was rejected by his time. A writer who wants to be popular in his time must make concessions.

Bierce made none. With a touch of the sensuous, of the best sort of sentimentalism, of poetic craftiness, Bierce might have been the American Maupassant. He fails to be that, and yet remains in the first half-dozen writers of the short story in his own country. Isolated, too bitterly uncompromising to be popular, too mercurial to be measured and ticketed, Bierce is the connecting link between Poe and the American short story of to-day.

There are many Americas, and it is significant that neither American literature in general nor the American short story in particular has yet produced a voice that could speak for the whole continent. Perhaps it never will, and from Sarah Orne Jewett onwards there have fortunately always been isolated writers who have seen that their strength would lie in a devotion to one specified, and even narrow, regional scene.

American writers were slow to accept the necessity of narrowing their field of vision, yet in Sarah Orne Jewett, born a hundred years before regionalism became a national cliché, they were offered their first example. Miss Jewett has been accepted as the epitome of New England Puritanism, exactly as Miss Mitford and Mrs. Gaskell have been accepted as the expression of English Victorianism. Yet Miss Jewett herself nicely pointed out " that she was descended from English cavalier, not from Puritan stock." [1] Her art, because of a certain correctitude in its finished simplicity, seems to have inspired a stereotyped line of praise : charming, fragrant, delicate, modest, delightful. Her stories undoubtedly

[1] Edward Garnett : footnote, p. 192, *Friday Nights* (Cape)

possess these qualities, but they also undoubtedly possess something else. Of all the New England stories (no doubt charming, delicate, and modest too) produced by Miss Jewett's contemporaries, few, as Miss Willa Cather points out, are worth re-reading to-day. Behind Miss Jewett's stories, behind the charm and the fragrance and the delicacy, there is in fact a certain controlled rigidity of mind. " To note an artist's limitations," as Miss Cather remarks again, " is but to define his genius." [1] This is quite true ; but for an artist to note his own limitations, to accept them and to be content to work within them, is one way of rarefying that genius. Miss Jewett, recognizing that she knew nothing in the world better than the fisher-folk and farmers of New England and the countryside she had seen as a child from the seat of her father's buggy, intelligently accepted that limitation, knowing quite well that it might make her art provincial, and if she were not careful, parochial. In actual fact her art, steered by a mind that handled its material with what Edward Garnett called " a clearness of phrase almost French," is rarely in any such danger. It has the quality of a pastoral, for all its reticence and delicacy quite strong and realistic. It has the rare quality of paint translated to words.

Miss Jewett was lucky in possessing an essential gift of both writer and painter—a remarkable eye ; but she was still luckier in having the intelligence to write with that eye on the object. Her world, like Jane Austen's, was small, but, like Jane Austen, if she had chosen it herself

[1] Preface, *The Country of the Pointed Firs* (Travellers' Library) ·

she could hardly have been born into a world more aptly suited to her gift of interpretation. One cannot help feeling that Bierce, her contemporary, driven by a mind like an engine whose differentials were never quite working in harmony, would have been happier in another century. Not so Miss Austen or Miss Jewett. The accident of their date is so happy that their books give the impression sometimes—in Jane Austen's case quite often—of having chosen them rather than having been chosen by them. In the best sense of the word they are happy writers.

Turning from Miss Jewett to O. Henry is rather like turning from Jane Austen to some account of life in the gossip column of a Sunday newspaper. If Miss Jewett was the painter of a certain section of American life, O. Henry strikes one as being the itinerant photographer who buttonholes every passer-by in the street, wise-cracks him, snaps the camera, raises his hat and hands him the inevitable card. O. Henry has just the natural buoyancy, cheek, good-humour, wit, canny knowledge of humanity and its demands, and above all the tireless flamboyant gift of the gab that characterizes any seller of carpets, cure-alls, gold watches, and something-for-nothing in the open market place. O. Henry is not, and I think never was, a writer. He is a great showman who can talk the hind leg off a donkey and then proceed to sell the public that same donkey as a pedigree race-horse.

All this can be simply deduced from the stories. A life of hard facts, of great adversity, confirms it. O. Henry had little schooling, began work in a drug-store, was forced by ill-health to try his luck on a ranch, worked later in a bank, bought and edited a weekly paper, saw it fail, worked on another paper, and finished up in the Ohio State Penitentiary on a charge of embezzling funds. Contrast that with the calm fortunes of the Miss Austens and Miss Jewetts of this world. The wonder is not that O. Henry could not write, but perhaps that he was ever able to put a consecutive sentence together at all. Such adversity would have crushed into complete oblivion a lesser man, just as it might have turned a greater man into that all-American genius of realism for which America still waits. It simply made O. Henry into a trickster— the supreme example in the history of the short story of the showman " wrapping it up so that the fools don't know it."

But it would be the greatest injustice to O. Henry to leave it at that. The body of his work alone, the achievement of his colossal industry, entitles him to something more. His manipulation and marketing of a new type of story (in reality borrowed from others), whose chief effect was that of the surprise packet, entitles him to more again. For however you talk round O. Henry he still emerges, by his huge achievement and the immense popularity of his particular method, as an astonishingly persistent influence on the short story of almost every decade since his day.

O. Henry had many of the qualities that make a greater writer. His eye was excellent, and he was able to focus it on an immense variety of objects, and always, thanks to an immense experience, realistically ; he was tire-

lessly interested in people and could make people tirelessly interesting ; he had a certain sense of tragedy, a
deep if sentimental sympathy for the underdog, was at
his best a sublime humorist, and was blessed with that
peculiar faculty of being able to impress the flavour of
himself on the page. These qualities, backed by a
stronger attitude of mind, a certain relentlessness, might
have made O. Henry really great. They were backed
instead by a showman who was also a sentimentalist.
As a journalist O. Henry knew how to spread it on
and spread it out ; he knew all about the human touch ;
he knew, as Bret Harte did, all about the laughter behind
the tears. What his work never had was reticence or
delicacy ; his poetry was that of the journalist who,
unable to conceive a lyrical image and knowing that it
would be wasted anyway, reaches for the book of
Metaphors and Phrases. On anything like a real test his
work will fail because of a certain shallowness, the
eternal touch of the cheapjack who palms you off with
the imitation of the real thing.

Yet O. Henry, perhaps more than Maupassant, put
the short story on the map. His brand of goods tapped
a world market. And to-day you will still find him held
in affection, as much as esteem, by a great many people
who will not hear a word against his method and its
results. For this reason I must not overlook a certain
quality of lovableness about O. Henry—a quality well
seen, I think, in such a story as *The Cop and the Anthem*.
But that quality alone could not, and does not, account
for O. Henry's great popularity. That popularity sprang

from a conjuring trick—the story with the surprise—or trick-ending.

This was nothing new. Some use of it may be seen in Poe and Bierce, and a good deal of use of it may be seen in Bret Harte, who apparently failed to grasp its greatest possibilities, as may be seen in the anti-climax of the last six lines of *The Iliad of Sandy Bar*. But for some reason O. Henry's use of it captures the imagination not only of readers but also of writers, so that long after O. Henry's death writers like Maugham were still using it, though more perhaps on the Maupassant model than that of O. Henry. For to Maupassant, and not O. Henry, still belongs that supreme *tour de force* of surprise endings, *The Necklace*, in which the excellence and the limitation of the method can be perfectly seen. Maupassant's story of the woman who borrows a diamond necklace from a friend, loses it, buys another to replace it, and is condemned to ten years' suffering and poverty by the task of paying off the money, only to make the awful discovery at last that the original necklace was not diamond but paste—this story, dependent though it is for effect on the shock of the last line, differs in one extremely important respect from anything O. Henry ever did. For here, in *The Necklace*, trick and tragedy are one. By placing a certain strain on the credulity of the reader (why, one asks, was it not explained in the first place that the necklace was paste? or why, later, did not Madame Loisel make a clean breast of everything to a friend who had so much trusted her?), by the skilful elimination of probabilities, Maupassant is left holding a shocking and surprising card of which the reader is entirely ignorant. He is entirely ignorant, that is, *the first time*. Like a child who is frightened by the first sudden bo ! from round the corner, but knows all about it next time, the reader of *The Necklace* can never be tricked again. For Maupassant is bound to play that card, which is his only by a process of cheating, and having played it can never again repeat its devastating effect. In story-telling, as in parlour games, you can never hope to hoodwink the same person twice. It is only because of Maupassant's skilful delineation of Madame Loisel's tragedy that *The Necklace* survives as a credible piece of realism. Maupassant, the artist, was well aware that the trick alone is its own limitation ; O. Henry, the journalist, never was aware of it.

Yet by the use of the trick, by the telling of scores of stories solely for the point, the shock, or the witty surprise of the last line, O. Henry made himself famous and secured for himself a large body of readers. Apparently neither he nor they ever tired of this game of trick endings. Yet no one, so far as I know, has drawn attention to the technical excellence of O. Henry's trick beginnings. Mr. Ellery Sedgewick, following up his opinion that " a story is like a horse race, it is the start and finish that count most," goes on to say, " Of these two the beginning is the harder. I am not sure but it is the most difficult accomplishment in fiction."

O. Henry was well aware of that. In the market-place the cheap-jack is confronted with precisely the same difficulty—the problem of making the public listen, even of making it listen, if necessary, against its will, since the nicely wrapped-up ending is entirely useless if the beginning has failed to attract the customer. And in re-shaping the short story's beginning, in dispensing with its former leisureliness, its preliminary loquacity, and its well-balanced lead-up, O. Henry did a very considerable service to the short story. He recognized, as the following examples will show, the great value of an instant contact between reader and writer :

So I went to a doctor.
" How long has it been since you took alcohol into your system ? " he asked.

Finch keeps a hats-cleaned-by-electricity-while-you-wait establishment, nine feet by twelve, in Third Avenue. Once a customer, you are always his. I do not know his secret process, but every four days your hat needs to be cleaned again.

The trouble began in Laredo. It was the Leano Kid's fault, for he should have confined his habit of man-slaughter to Mexicans.

On his bench in Madison Square Soapy moved un-easily. When wild geese honk high of nights, and when women without sealskin coats grow kind to their husbands, and when Soapy moves uneasily on his bench in the park, you may know that winter is near at hand.

These are examples taken almost at random ; there are many others. O. Henry rarely fumbles the beginning, and when he does so it is invariably by the two pieces of fancy irresistible to the journalist of his type : a desire to be moral, a desire to show that he knows all about poetry. Otherwise he can show a series of masterly lessons not only in how to begin a story but, perhaps more important, when to begin.

As a humorist O. Henry stands in the true line of what appears to be an essentially American tradition—the tradition in which Leacock, Thurber, and Runyon are true-blood descendants. That tradition appears to be largely the expression of the wider American revolt against the heavier values so held in esteem in the Old World : pomposity, class distinction, dignity, family tradition, and indeed almost anything liable to be taken over-seriously. By taking such things as pompous family tradition and treating them with levity (as in Leacock) or by taking trivialities and treating them with a language mixed into an affected combination of the academic and the vernacular (as in Runyon), American writers produce a high contrast that is, as in Wodehouse, very funny. In this method O. Henry, who excelled in the use of both vernacular and a certain pompous brand of journalese, was bound to be a success.

But long before O. Henry's first volume, *Cabbages and Kings* (1904), America had thrown up a writer who may well have learned something from him, who was realist and humorist, who felt the same attraction for the life of East Side New York and Latin America, who handled vernacular joyously, and who possessed in a high degree the final quality that O. Henry lacked—for " here came a boy," says Mr. Thomas Beer,[1] " whose visual sense was unique in American writing, and whose mind by some inner process had stripped itself of all respect for those prevalent theories which have cursed the national fiction "—here, in short, arrived an ironist and a poet, Stephen Crane.

In the very early nineteen-twenties, as a boy of sixteen or seventeen, I picked up a story of Crane's called *Five White Mice*, and was electrified and troubled by that curious feeling, which you get sometimes on hearing a piece of music, of renewed acquaintance, of having taken the thing out of the storage of my own mind. I have no doubt now that this was purely the result of a certain quality of inevitability in Crane, a quality found less in prose literature than in poetry and music, where again and again the order of words and sounds has the air, most notably in Shakespeare and Mozart, of having been preordained. " An artist," says Miss Elizabeth Bowen in a study of Jane Austen,[2] " can never be fully conscious," but in Stephen Crane, author of some of the most remarkable short stories in American literature, you have an example of an artist who was really not conscious at all. " An artist, to be effective," says Miss Bowen again, " has to be half-critic. Fancy and reason ought to have equal strength." Crane's genius, on the other hand, was entirely intuitive. He apparently never knew,

[1] Thomas Beer : *Stephen Crane : A Study* (Heinemann)
[2] Derek Verschoyle : ed. *English Novelists* (Chatto and Windus)

as Conrad once remarked, how good his best work was. He arrived (and the phenomenon is by no means rare in American literature) fully equipped ; he had no need to improve, to work " forward on the lines of patient, ascending effort " ; it was his tragedy that he began at the highest point of his achievement and thereafter could only descend.

Crane's life and work have, in fact, all the picturesque and tragic qualities of the story of genius. In 1892 he wrote, in two days, a long-short story called *Maggie*. It is the story of a prostitute. Never, perhaps, in the history of the American short story has a story of a prostitute been written at a more inopportune moment. Fearlessly honest, almost cruelly realistic, without a touch of " visible sentiment," it gave both Crane's friends and the editors of the day an attack of the horrors. Up to that moment no one in American literature had done anything like it. Crane simply cut off from life—or rather the section of it called the Bowery—a lump of raw meat and slapped it down on the pages with neither dressing nor garnish, asking later of horrified editors, " You mean the story's too honest ? " Crane, like all writers who desire simply to set down what they see as truthfully as possible, must have been inexpressibly shocked to find that there was any other viewpoint or standard. What he had done must have seemed to him, as to most rebel writers, a very natural thing. The Bowery was full of drunks, prostitutes, crooks, loafers, and everything else ; they talked a strong unacademic language (" Look at deh dirt what yeh done me. Deh ol' woman 'ill be trowin' fits ") ; they lived a life of saloons and debt, violence and stench, tears and trouble. Crane simply set it down, doing more or less what someone else forty years later was to do, and be applauded for, in *Dead End*. To-day *Maggie*, though its essential qualities and naturalism and truth remain completely undated, has little power to shock. In 1892 Crane took it from publisher to publisher as if it were a bomb. Finally, in despair and with astonishing ignorance, Crane borrowed a thousand dollars and paid for the publication of the book himself. "The bill for printing eleven hundred copies was $869, and Appletons tell me that the printer must have made about $700 out of me. . . . A firm of religious and medical printers did me the dirt." A year after *Maggie* was written Crane had succeeded in disposing of a hundred copies of his mustard-covered volume at 50 cents a time, and thereafter entered "that period of starvation so much admired in the history of artists by comfortable critics."

It is now, of course, an old story that W. D. Howells went "sedately mad" over *Maggie*, and proceeded to champion Crane. This helped to make Crane's future, but it was not until Crane, partly it seems out of a bravado to do better than Zola and partly out of a worship of *War and Peace*, wrote *The Red Badge of Courage*, that things began to happen. That short novel is a picture, as realistic in its way as *Maggie*, of the American Civil War. It has some of the sardonic, brilliant, and embittered quality of Bierce ; but what makes it exceptional is that though the Civil War was legally if not

emotionally ended in 1865, Crane was not born until
1871. By an intensified imaginative approach Crane
wrote a novel that could scarcely have been more real
if he had fought in the conflict. It seemed like a piece
of factual reporting inspired by memory. It had great
success—but, what is more significant, Crane's only
success in the novel-form. Subsequently his very great
natural gift of visual writing was to express itself in the
form for which it was inevitably adapted. In a couple
of dozen stories Crane was to impress on the short story
of his time, and indeed of all time, a new poetic irony.

What was Crane's method ? Sometimes I doubt if
he ever had a method, except that of direct transposition.
Forty years after Crane's death Mr. Christopher Isherwood is expressing many a writer's feeling and attitude
with the significant words, " Some day all this will have
to be developed, carefully printed, fixed." [1] From that
method Crane's method differed only in the speed of the
recorded performance ; there was no " some day," no
sort of recollection in tranquillity. Long before the
motion-picture camera shot the Bowery or the cacti of
Mexico, Crane had shot them with an eye mounted on
a swivel, so that his stories are made up, like a film, of a
series of selected illuminatory shots, often of startling
metaphorical vividness. But like the camera, Crane
reflected the surface of things ; the eye was so swift in
its reflexes that the mind behind it apparently had no
time to check, re-direct or re-shape the image it recorded.
Such a powerful natural gift inevitably imposed its own

[1] Christopher Isherwood : *Good-bye to Berlin* (Hogarth)

limitations ; the moment it ceased to function, for whatever reason, Crane's art became, as in the later novels
and stories, as commonplace as calico :

> Although Whilomville was in no sense a summer
> resort, the advent of the warm season meant much to
> it, for then came visitors from the city—people of
> considerable confidence—alighting upon their country
> cousins.[1]

The method—if there is a method—is that of any
tenth-rate provincial reporter without the wit to de-
termine whether what he is doing is good or bad. To
go back to almost any early sentence of Crane is to
discover incredible contrast :

> The sun swung steadily up the sky, and they knew
> it was broad day because the colour of the sea
> changed from slate to emerald green, streaked with
> amber lights, and the foam was like trembling snow.[2]

The sharp colouring, the vivid, awakening effect, are
qualities that touch every page of this volume, *The Open
Boat*, with a strange brilliance of personal tone. Here
the Mexican stories are like flashes of sombre, tropical
paint ; *The Pace of Youth* is a perfect gem of comic
spontaneity ; in *Death and the Child* all the malignant
terror and stupidity of war is shown up in a way that
seems even more bitterly true to-day than when it was

[1] Stephen Crane : *Whilomville Stories* (Harper and Orn, 1900)
[2] Stephen Crane : *The Open Boat* (Heinemann, 1898)

written ; in *The Bride Comes to Yellow Sky* one is irresistibly reminded of certain well-directed Westerns, notably passages of *Stage-Coach*, in which a quality of poised and sinister tension is remarkably handled. In all these stories, and their companions, Crane is working with pictures ; he is painting rather than writing ; and no other writer in the whole of American literature, up to the end of the nineteenth century, can challenge his natural gift of swift impressionism.

Indeed Crane, like Bierce, belongs to to-day rather than to the day before yesterday. His method is closely aligned with the method now more and more in contemporary use ; the method by which a story is told not by the carefully engineered plot but by the implication of certain isolated incidents, by the capture and significant arrangement of casual, episodic moments. It is the method by which the surface, however seemingly trivial or unimportant, is recorded in such a way as to interpret the individual emotional life below. Crane handed the basic point of that method to a generation that was not ready for it. Dying at the turn of the century, exhausted by disease, by over-work as a war-correspondent, and by a curious romantic passion for living grandly, Crane seems for a moment to mark the end of an age. In reality, I think, he anticipates one. He anticipates a generation of prose-writers who, in another age, would have found a more natural expression in lyric poetry and who now find, in the short story, their nearest working medium ; he is the forerunner of writers who replace the use of the artificially concocted situation with the record of life seen at first hand, the picture "developed, carefully printed, fixed" and unmarred by the professional touch-up of the studio.

Before the hand of Crane was linked up to that of Sherwood Anderson in the nineteen-twenties, the history of the American short story became in fact a desert of immense aridity. Obstinately influenced by O. Henry and Kipling, seduced by the dollar-value of the machine-made product, writers debased the whole form to its lowest level. "Men and women," says Mr. E. J. O'Brien, "were two-dimensional, were silhouettes cut out of coloured paper. They solved artificial dilemmas. A progressive weakening of subject was noticeable from year to year. The emphasis on the formal pattern became more and more pronounced. The story tended to become more and more machine made. There was a formal code, Augustan in its rigour, and if the rule were followed the story was thought to be good." [1] In this period of the American short story there is no regionalism, little poetry, no experiment ; no writer comparable with Bierce, Miss Jewett, or Crane emerges ; in the complacency of the time there is no suspicion that the art will one day, in the hands of Katherine Mansfield, be given new and popular delicacy or, in the hands of Hemingway, torn completely to shreds and reshaped. We are confronted with something which so resembles a balance-sheet that it is a relief, at last, to turn to Europe again.

[1] E. J. O'Brien ; intro. *Best Short Stories, 1930* : *American* (Cape)

CHAPTER IV

TCHEHOV AND MAUPASSANT

IN nineteenth-century America the short story took a series of halting steps forward, its performance rather resembling that of a child learning to walk. If at times it walked badly it could at least be said to be walking by itself; if it did not walk far it could also be said that vast continents are not explored in a day. It needs little perception to note the main defects of the American short story from Poe to Crane. It was often raw, facile, journalistic, prosy, cheap ; it was unexperimental, and, except in rare instances, unpoetical. It was all these things, and much more ; so that beside the European (not English) short story of the same day it appears to suffer from one huge and common defect. It lacked culture.

In Europe, on the other hand, culture rose readily and naturally to the top of artistic life like so much cream. By contrast with the saloon-bar back-cloths of Bret Harte, the Bowery of Crane, the embittered etchings of Bierce, the literary life and output of Europe appeared richly civilized, smooth, and settled. In France Flaubert could spend years polishing and perfecting the periods of *Madame Bovary* ; in Russia Turgenev and Tolstoy were bringing the art of the novel to the state where it was becoming what has been called " the great means of cosmopolitan culture " ; these writers worked in, depicted, and appealed to a more or less settled civilization, with more or less fixed boundaries. In America the writers of the day appear to suffer from a certain common, and quite natural, bewilderment ; half their continent is undeveloped, much unexplored ; they have not found their feet, and they give the natural impression of needing not only a pen but a compass in their hands. The literature of that America is amateurish, unorganized, still in its working clothes ; that of Europe is civilized, centralized, well dressed.

Under these circumstances it would be strange if Europe had not something to offer, in the short-story as well as in literature generally, that America did not and could not possess. It would be surprising indeed if it had not produced at least one short-story writer greater than Poe or O. Henry. It did in fact produce several ; but from many distinguished names two stand out as the pillars of the entire structure of the modern short story : Guy de Maupassant, born in 1850, and Anton Pavlovitch Tchehov, born ten years later.

During recent years it has become the fashion to divide both exponents and devotees of the short story into two camps, Maupassant fans on the one side, Tchehovites on the other. On the one side we are asked to contemplate the decisive virtues of the clear, acid, realistic straight-forwardness of the French mind, which tells a story with masterly simplicity and naturalism, producing such masterpieces as *Boule de Suif*; on the other hand we are asked to marvel at the workings of a mind which saw life as it were obliquely, unobtrusively, touching it almost by remote control, telling its stories by an apparently aimless arrangement of casual incidents and producing such masterpieces as *The Darling*. From one side emerges a certain derision for the peasant vulgarity of the man who was preoccupied with the fundamental passions ; from the other comes the tired sneer for the man in whose stories nothing ever happens except conversations, the drinking of tea and vodka, and an infinite number of boring resolutions about the soul and work that never gets done. To some, Maupassant's stories leave a nasty taste in the mouth ; to others Tchehov's are unintelligible. To some the Maupassant method of story-telling is the method *par excellence* ; to others there is nothing like Tchehov. This sort of faction even found an exponent in Mr. Somerset Maugham, who devoted a large part of a preface to extolling Maupassant at the expense of Tchehov, for no other reason apparently than that he had found in Maupassant a more natural model and master.

Odd as it may seem to the adherent of these two schools, there are many readers, as well as writers, by whom Tchehov and Maupassant are held in equal affection and esteem. Among these I like to number myself. I confess I cannot decide and never have been able to decide whether *Boule de Suif* or *The Steppe* is the finer story ; whether *Mademoiselle Fifi* is superior to *The Party* ; whether *Maison Tellier* is greater than *Ward No. 6*. In admiring them all I have learned from them

74

almost equally. For me Tchehov has had many lessons ;
but it is significant to note that I learned none of them
until I had learned others from Maupassant. I recall a
period when both were held for hours under the
microscope ; and in consequence I have never had any
sympathy with the mind that is enthusiastic for one but
impatient of the other. Much of their achievement and
life bears an astonishing similarity ; the force of their
influence, almost equally powerful, has extended farther
than that of any other two short-story writers in the
world. Both were popular in their lifetime ; both were
held in sedate horror by what are known as decent
people. Tchehov, they said, would die in a ditch, and
it is notable that Maupassant still holds a lurid attraction
for the ill-balanced.

The differences of Tchehov and Maupassant have
therefore, I think, been over-laboured, and in no point
so much as that of technique. Their real point of
difference is indeed fundamental, and arises directly not
from what they did, but from what they were. For in
the final analysis it is not the writer that is important,
but the man ; not the technician but the character.
Technical competence, even what appears to be revolutionary technical competence, can be, and in fact always
is, in some way acquired ; and since writing is an
artificial process there is no such thing as a " born
writer." The technician responds to analysis, to certain
tests of the critical laboratory. The personality behind
the technician, imposing itself upon the shaping of every
technical gesture and yet itself elusive of analysis, is the

thing for which there exists no abiding or common formula. There is no sort of prescription which, however remorselessly followed, will produce a preconceived personality.

Thus Tchehov and Maupassant, so alike in many things, are fundamentally worlds apart. Almost each point of similarity, indeed, throws into relief a corresponding point of difference. Both, for example, sprang from peasant stock; both excelled in the delineation of peasant types. But whereas Maupassant's peasants give the repeated impression of being an avaricious, hard, logical, meanly passionate, and highly suspicious race, Tchehov's give the impression of good-humoured laziness, dreamy ignorance, kindliness, of being the victims of fatalism, of not knowing quite what life is all about. Again, one of their favourite themes was the crushing or exploitation of a kindly, innocent man by a woman of strong and remorseless personality; in Maupassant the woman would be relentlessly drawn, sharp and heartless as glass; in Tchehov the woman would be seen indirectly through the eyes of a secondary, softer personality, perhaps the man himself. Similarly both liked to portray a certain type of weak, stupid, thoughtless woman, a sort of yes-woman who can unwittingly impose tragedy or happiness on others. Maupassant had no patience with the type; but in Olenka, in *The Darling*, it is precisely a quality of tender patience, the judgment of the heart and not the head, that gives Tchehov's story its effect of uncommon understanding and radiance. Both writers knew a very wide world teeming with a vast number of types : not only peasants but aristocrats, artisans, school teachers, government clerks, prostitutes, ladies of the bored middle-class, waiters, doctors, lovers, priests, murderers, children, thieves, the very poor and the very ignorant, artists, the very rich and the very ignorant, students, business men, lawyers, adolescents, the very old, and so on. Their clientele was enormous ; yet the attitude of Maupassant towards that clientele gives the impression, constantly, of being that of a lawyer ; his interest and sympathy are detached, cold, objectively directed ; the impression is often that, in spite of his energy and carefully simulated interest, he is really wondering if there is not something he can get out of it. Is the woman frail ? Has the man money ? It is not uncommon for Maupassant to laugh at his people, or to give the impression of despising them, both effects being slightly repellent. " What they are doing," he seems to say, " is entirely their own responsibility. I only present them as they are." Tchehov, on the other hand, without closely identifying himself with his characters, sometimes in an unobtrusive way assumes responsibility. His is by no means the attitude of the lawyer, but of the doctor—very naturally, since his first profession was medicine—holding the patient's hand by the bedside. His receptivity, his capacity for compassion, are both enormous. Of his characters he seems to say, " I know what they are doing is their own responsibility. But how did they come to this, how did it happen ? There may be some trivial thing that will explain." That triviality, discovered, held for a moment in the light, is the key to Tchehov's emotional solution. In Maupassant's case the importance of that key would have been inexorably driven home ; but as we turn to ask of Tchehov if we have caught his meaning aright it is to discover that we must answer that question for ourselves—for Tchehov has gone.

Inquisitiveness, the tireless exercise of a sublime curiosity about human affairs, is one of the foremost essentials of the writer. It is a gift which both Maupassant and Tchehov possessed in abundance. But both possessed, in a very fine degree, a second dominant quality, a sort of corrective, which may be defined as a refined sense of impatience. One of the directest results of inquisitiveness is garrulity ; perhaps the worst of society's minor parasites are not nosey-parkers, but those who will not stop talking. We are all gossips by nature ; it is an excellent gift to know when to hold the tongue. Too few writers have a sense of personal impatience with their own voice, but it was a sixth sense to Maupassant and Tchehov, as it is in some degree to every short-story writer of importance at all. Both knew to perfection when they had said enough ; an acute instinct continually reminded them of the fatal tedium of explanation, of going on a second too long. In Tchehov this sense of impatience, almost a fear, caused him frequently to stop speaking, as it were, in mid-air. It was this which gave his stories an air of remaining unfinished, of leaving the reader to his own explanations, of imposing on each story's end a note of suspense so abrupt and yet refined that it produced on the reader an effect of delayed shock.

It is very unlikely, of course, that Tchehov was wholly unaware of this gift, or that he did not use it consciously. Yet if writers are only partly conscious of the means by which they create their effects, as it seems fairly obvious they are, then what appears to be one of Tchehov's supreme technical gifts may only be the natural manifestation of something in the man. From his letters you get the impression that Tchehov was a man of the highest intelligence, personal charm, and sensibility, a man who was extremely wise and patient with the failings of others, but who above all hated the thought of boring others by the imposition of his own personality. Most of his life he was a sick man, deprived for long intervals of the intellectual stimulus and gaiety he loved so much, yet he never gives an impression of self-pity but rather of self-effacement. He was beautifully modest about himself, and " during the last six years of his life—growing weaker in body and stronger in spirit—taking a marvellously simple, wise and beautiful attitude to his bodily dissolution, because ' God has put a bacillus into me.' " [1] Contrast that quality with the story of Maupassant who, at the height of his success, used ostentatiously to bank his large weekly cheque at a certain provincial bank, holding it so that those at his elbow might not miss the size of the amount.

Tchehov's charm, the light balance of his mind, and his natural gift of corrective impatience were bound to be reflected in the style he used, and it is impossible to

[1] Constance Garnett : intro. trans. *Letters of Anton Pavlovitch Tchehov to Olga Knijper* (Chatto and Windus)

imagine Tchehov writing in that heavy, indigestible, cold-pork fashion so characteristic of much English fiction of his own day. In describing the countryside, the scenery, the weather, for example, Tchehov again exhibits a natural impatience with the obvious prevailing mode of scenic description ; in his letters he shows this to be a conscious impatience, and condemns what he calls anthropomorphism : " the frequent personification . . . when the sea breathes, the sky gazes, the steppe barks, Nature whispers, speaks, mourns and so on . . . Beauty and expressiveness in Nature are attained only by simplicity, by some such simple phrase as ' The sun set,' ' It was dark,' ' It began to rain ' and so on," [1] To Maupassant the necessity of creating effects by the use of the most natural simplicity must also have been obvious. In that sense, perhaps more than any other, Maupassant and Tchehov are much alike. Both are masters in what might be called the art of distillation, of compressing into the fewest, clearest possible syllables the spirit and essence of a scene. Both were capable in a very fine degree of a highly sensuous reaction to place. Both, more important still, were capable of transmitting it to the page :

> The tall grass, among which the yellow dandelions rose up like streaks of yellow light, was of a vivid fresh spring green.

> Beyond the poplar stretches of wheat extended like a bright yellow carpet from the road to the top of the hills.

[1] Constance Garnett : trans. *Letters of Anton Tchehov*

Of these two descriptions, so simple and yet so vivid pictorially and atmospherically, each creating its effect in the same number of words, it would be hard to say at random which was Tchehov and which Maupassant : the effect in both is beautifully and swiftly transmitted ; no fuss, no grandiose staying of the scene, no elaborate signalling that the reader is about to be the victim of a description of nature. The words are like clear, warm, delicate paint.

Contrast their effect with what Mr. E. M. Forster has called "Scott's laborious mountains and carefully scooped out glens and carefully ruined abbeys," [1] or with Hardy, who was writing side by side with Maupassant and Tchehov, as he struggles for six pages to convey the gloomy impression of Egdon Heath :

It was a spot which returned upon the memory of those who loved it with an aspect of peculiar and kindly congruity. Smiling champaigns of flowers and fruit hardly do this, for they are permanently harmonious only with the existence of better reputation as to its issues than the present.

What are we listening to ?—for it is clear at once that we are listening and not looking—a guide-book ? a sermon ? a windy report ? Hardy is not painting a picture, but is talking about what he sincerely believes to be a description of a picture. His failure is highly pompous, entirely uninstructive, and unconsciously

[1] E. M. Forster : *Aspects of the Novel* (Arnold)

81

amusing. It is not even the failure of a man trying to paint a small canvas with a whitewash brush ; it is the failure of a man trying to paint a picture with a dictionary.

Neither Maupassant nor Tchehov was ever guilty of this mistake ; neither was a dictionary man. From both one gets the impression that they might never have kept such a thing as a dictionary in the house. The style of both conforms consistently to a beautiful standard of simplicity—direct, apparently artless, sometimes almost child-like, but never superficial. In Maupassant it is a simplicity that is brittle, swift, logical, brilliant, and hard as a gem ; in Tchehov it is clear, casual, conversational, sketchy, and delicate as lace. Both, however, were capable of genuine elaboration, as and when the theme demanded it, so that both are masters in a wide range not only of subjects, moods, and pictures, but of forms also. In such stories as *The Steppe, Ward No. 6, The Black Monk, Yvette, The Story of a Farm Girl*, and so on, they are masters of the longer story ; at the same time both brought to the very short sketch, the significant impressionistic trifle of a few pages, an artistry it had never known.

It is indisputable that both were great writers, but if we look for a common and insistent characteristic, or lack of one, which sets them apart from English writers of their own time, we are faced with the fact that they were not gentlemen. In further discussing Scott, Mr. Forster makes the point that he lacks passion and " only has a temperate heart and gentlemanly feelings." But if there is one thing that Maupassant and Tchehov possess, though in highly contrasting forms, it is passion ; and if there was one condition which neither imposed on his work it was gentlemanly feelings. To the English novel a certain moral attitude, or at very least the recognition of the governing force of morality, has always seemed indispensable. One of its most luscious crops is that of the bitter fruits of sin. Not until Samuel Butler turned up, with *The Way of All Flesh*, had any writer of the nineteenth century the courage to suggest that the fruits of sin are more often than not quite pleasant enough. Neither Maupassant nor Tchehov had much truck with sin ; both declined to entangle themselves or their characters in the coils of an artificial and contemporary morality ; both set down life and people as nearly as possible as they saw them, pure or sinful, pleasant or revolting, admirable or vicious, feeling that that process needed neither explanation nor apology. To the old, old criticism that such a process produced a literature that was disgusting Tchehov rightly and properly replied, "No literature can outdo real life in its cynicism" ; and went on :

To a chemist nothing on earth is unclean. A writer must be as objective as a chemist, he must lay aside his personal subjective standpoint and must understand that muck-heaps play a very respectable part in the landscape, and that the inherent bad passions are as inherent as the good ones.

In short, all life is the writer's province ; never mind

about gentlemanly feelings : a view with which Maupassant, it is quite clear, would have been in firm and complete agreement. Like Burns, indeed, Maupassant and Tchehov pleaded for the acceptance of human frailty as a condition of their work—the acceptance of the fact that, as Mr. Edward Garnett pointed out, " people cannot be other than what they are." [1] In all of what he had to say about this frailty Tchehov was never cynical; he brought to its interpretation qualities of tenderness, patience, a kind of humorously wise understanding, and what has been described as " candour of soul," a quality which, it has been suggested, was by no means exclusive to Tchehov, but was a virtue common to all the greatest Russian writers from Pushkin down to Gorki. Maupassant had none of that Russian candour of soul, but rather excelled in candour of mind. Where he was cynical, Tchehov was merely sceptical, and what Tchehov was really remarkable for, it seems to me, was not so much candour of soul as greatness of heart. Mr. Middleton Murry has called it, rather characteristically perhaps, pureness of heart—" and in that," he says, " though we dare not analyse it further, lies the secret of his greatness as a writer and his present importance to ourselves." [2]

This was written twenty years ago, when Tchehov's extreme modernity could further inspire Mr. Murry to remark that " to-day we begin to perceive how intimately Tchehov belongs to us ; to-morrow we may feel

[1] Edward Garnett : " Tchehov and His Art " from *Friday Nights* (Cape)
[2] J. Middleton Murry : *Aspects of Literature* (Collins)

how infinitely he is in advance of us." [1] To-day Tchehov
still exercises a vital influence on the short story, and
still, in many ways, seems more in advance of us than
almost any other exponent of it, including Maupassant.
It seems remarkable, for example, that Tchehov was at
work when Bret Harte was at work, and died indeed
only two years after him. Does the author of *Mliss*
exercise a powerful influence on contemporary thought
or writing to-day ? Does he seem in advance of us ?
Yet the work of writers, once printed, does not change.
The words that Bret Harte and Tchehov put down on the
page in 1896, for example, are the words that still appear
on the page to-day. Yet something has changed, obviously very radically and very drastically, and if that
something is not the work it can only be the standards,
the judgment, and the world of those who read the
work. Time is the inexorable acid test. In a few years
it eats away the meretricious exterior veneer of writers
like Bret Harte, who thereafter go through a rapid
process known as dating, and yet leaves the delicate
surfaces of such writers as Turgenev, Sarah Orne Jewett,
Tchehov, Maupassant, and so on untouched. Time knows
no standards of criticism, and yet is the definitive test.
" If a man writes clearly enough," says Hemingway,
" anyone can see if he fakes." [2] Exactly : if there is a
subtler kind of faking it is simply a question of time, as
Hemingway goes on to point out, before the fake is discovered. So after all, perhaps, the so-called modernity
of Tchehov, and for that matter of Maupassant

[1] *Ibid.*   [2] Ernest Hemingway : *Death in the Afternoon* (Cape)

too, has nothing to do with pureness of heart. It has nothing to do with technique, except in so far as technique is another word for control. It arises perhaps from something very old, very simple, and yet not at all simple of achievement : the setting down of the truth as you see it and feel it, without tricks or sham or fake, so that it never appears out-dated by fashion or taste but remains the truth, or at least some part of the truth, for as long as the truth can matter.

Both Maupassant and Tchehov strove for that result ; both achieved it with a remarkable degree of success. The artist who fakes must initially regard his audience with some kind of contempt which is inseparable from any such attitude as " wrapping it up so that the fools don't know it." Neither Maupassant nor Tchehov wrote for an audience of fools ; neither did any wrapping up—rather the contrary. Yet if we look for another point of difference between them, it is that Tchehov's estimation of his audience rose a shade or two higher than Maupassant's. Tchehov, taking it for granted that his audience could fill in the detail and even the colour of a partially stated picture, wrote consistently on a fine line of implication. Maupassant rather tended to fill in the picture ; his natural distrust of humanity's intelligence inevitably extended to his readers. In consequence he is more direct ; the colours are filled in ; his points are clearly made ; the reader is left far less to his own devices. Maupassant seems to say, in the logical, economical way of a French peasant: "Having gone to all the trouble to prepare the ingredients and make the dish

I'll see that the eating of it isn't left to chance." Tchehov,
on the other hand, walks out before the end of the meal,
completely confident in the intelligence and ability of
his reader to finish things for himself.

This, of course, is entirely responsible for the most
constant of criticisms of Tchehov—that nothing ever
happens. The truth is that always, in Tchehov, a great
deal happens : not always on the page or during the
scene or during the present. Events or happenings are
implied ; they happen " off " ; they are hinted at, not
stated ; most important of all, they go on happening
after the story has ended. The reader who complains
that nothing happens is in reality uttering a criticism of
himself; the " nothing happens " is unfortunately in
his own mind. Tchehov has supplied certain apparently
trivial outlines which, if properly filled in, will yield
a picture of substance and depth, and has done the reader
the honour of believing that he is perceptive enough to
fill in the very substance that is not stated. Each reader
will fill in more or less of the picture, according to the
measure of his own perception and sensibility. But
the man who can fill in nothing and then hurls back at
Tchehov the charge that "nothing ever happens" is
simply turning Tchehov's generous estimate of himself
into an insult of Tchehov.

Perhaps we can look at a typical example of Tchehov's
method of implication, a story in which " nothing
happens." Take a very short one, *The Schoolmistress*.
What happens in it ?—*i.e.* what happens that can be set
down as so much co-ordinated material and physical

action ? The answer is that a schoolmistress who has been thirteen years in her post at an outlying village goes to town to fetch her salary ; as she is driving back she is overtaken by a rich, rather intelligent and handsome neighbour who rides part of the way with her, says a few trivial things and then says good-bye ; there follows a short argument with some peasants, and just before the story ends she sees the man once again as her horses wait for the road-barrier to be raised at the railway level crossing. That is all that can be called action ; the man, the driver of the cart, the peasants, and the charming state of the April weather are all briefly described. But there is no swift action, no dynamic impact of events, no runaway horse, no pursuit, no fainting, no dramatic rescue. The reader who seeks these things must feel that this is tiresome indeed. What, then, is the story about ?

The reader himself must supply that answer. Tchehov's story is not labelled True Love, Heartache, Disappointment, or A Tragic Woman ; it is not a public garden, as some stories are, with sign-posts saying To the Lake, To the Fairy Garden, and finally Exit. Tchehov does not label ; he does not point and push. He shows the schoolmistress thinking of her home in Moscow, her mother, " the aquarium with little fish . . . the sound of the piano " ; he shows her thinking again of her life as a schoolmistress, the inconvenience, discomfort, boredom, loneliness. The two lives, the real and the remembered, are thrown together, as they so often are in one's own experience, suddenly fused. Of the remembered life the cultured man Hanov, who is himself going to seed through loneliness and unhappy marriage, is a sort of real but unattainable symbol. As Tchehov unfolds these thoughts, the boundaries of the story gradually widen, until what appears to be a series of casual notes about a trivial journey becomes a universal tragedy of misplaced lives, of frustration, of "the happiness that would never be." When the story ends, Hanov and the schoolmistress step out of it into independent life. Presented as individuals, they emerge as figures of universality; and though we are touched by what happens to them within the limits of the story, it is the thought of what happens to them beyond these limits that moves us more deeply still.

That is something of what Tchehov is aiming at. To explain it, to subject it to a process of analysis, is really to destroy its living tissues. It is rather like dissecting a bird in order to solve the secrets of flight. In dissection, magic is lost.

Tchehov, therefore, places immense responsibility on the reader. Gifted with a finely graduated measure of sensibility, perception, and understanding, the reader will not fail. But where sensibility is dead and the reader cursed by a kind of short-sightedness, the charge of "greyness" and "nothing ever happens" is bound automatically to follow. Tchehov's method is therefore a risky one, partly because what Tchehov supplies is a negative that needs an equal positive to give it life, and the chances are that it may never get that positive; and partly for another reason. Supposing Tchehov's exposure to have been wrongly done, too seriously for example, and supposing the reader offers a response that is not seriously conceived ? In a moment Tchehov's serious beautiful picture produces exactly the reverse of Tchehov's intention ; it evokes, and is destroyed by, laughter.

This is the risk Tchehov ran in hundreds of stories. As a perfectly conscious writer he recognized it and insulated himself against it in the only possible way, by his own sense of humour. In a preface to Ernest Hemingway's *Torrents of Spring*, a parody of Sherwood Anderson, Mr. David Garnett [1] remarks how Anderson, in *Dark Laughter*, pushed his style to a degree of over-simplified affectation that produced an effect entirely opposite to the serious one intended. Even to Hemingway, at that time something of a devotee of Anderson, *Dark Laughter* was altogether too much. To parody it was the only corrective Hemingway could apply, and to do so was, in one way, a courageous thing, for in parodying Anderson Hemingway was also parodying himself. But it was better to have done that consciously, as Hemingway well knew, than to have gone on doing it unconsciously for the rest of his life.

Tchehov, of course, could be parodied, and no doubt could have parodied himself. Parody is one of the rewards of the highly individual writer. Self-applied, it is a corrective. To a tragic view of life (which he felt that no literature could outdo in cynicism) Tchehov was fortunate enough to be able to apply a constant corrective in the form of humour. Beginning as an author of comic sketches written for funny papers, Tchehov was only

[1] Ernest Hemingway : intro. *Torrents of Spring* (Cape)

with some difficulty persuaded by Grignovitch to take himself and his work more seriously. Luckily he never learnt that lesson thoroughly, and throughout his work the sly glance of corrective humour keeps breaking in. Tchehov, indeed, might be studied as a humorist. He delights in the farcical situation, the burlesque of life ; he loves to play skittles with pomposity, dignity, and the top-heaviness of mankind generally ; he adores the opportunity for discovering that the most impressive characters in life often wear false noses. Yet this humour is never mean ; throughout the whole of Tchehov there is not an echo of a single vinegary sneer. The qualities that colour his tragic view of life also colour his humorous view of it : charitableness, compassion, gentle irony, a kind of patient detachment. Tchehov had no judgment to pass, through either humour or tragedy, on the most ridiculous or the most depraved of his fellow-men. In the face of the appalling forces that shape lives Tchehov offered no condemnation. He seems rather to have felt that it was remarkable that mankind emerged as well as it did.

As compared with Maupassant, Tchehov will always, I think, seem the slightly more " advanced " and difficult writer. Maupassant, guided by more logical forces, left nothing to chance. Like all writers working within prescribed limits, he was fully aware of the value of a thing implied. By implying something, rather than stating it, a writer saves words, but he also runs the risk that his implication may never get home. That risk, in a very logical French way, Maupassant was less prepared to take than Tchehov. His pictures are more solidly built up ; he knows that faces, actions, manners, even the movements of hands and ways of walking are keys to human character ; in addition to that he takes a sensuous delight in physical shape, physical response, physical beauty, physical ugliness and behaviour; you can see that nothing delights him so much as a world of flesh and trees, clothes and food, leaves and limbs ; in describing such things, as he did so well, he was partially satisfying his own sensuous appetite. That fact gives his every material and physical description a profound flavour. When Maupassant talks of sweat you not only see sweat but you feel it and smell it ; when he describes a voluptuous and seductive woman the page itself seems to quiver sensuously. He knew, far better even than Tchehov, which words time and association have most heavily saturated with colour, scent, taste, and strength of emotional suggestion, and it is that knowledge, or instinct, and his skilful use of it, that constitutes one of his most powerful attributes as a writer.

For these reasons Maupassant's appeal will always be more direct and immediate, less subtle and oblique, than Tchehov's. He will always appear to be the greater story-teller, working as he does in the order of physical, emotional, and spiritual appeal. For even if a reader should miss the spiritual touch of a Maupassant story, and even the least subtle of its emotional implications, the physical character of the story would remain to give him a pleasure comparable to that of a woman who has nothing but a physical charm.

This is not of course quite as Maupassant intended.

For a Maupassant story is as closely co-ordinated as one of Tchehov ; ingredients in it cannot or should not be picked out singly and sampled to the exclusion of others ; you cannot pick out the choice morsels of passion and leave the unpleasant lumps of inhumanity, meanness, cruelty, deceit, and falsity which are so important a part of the Maupassant offering. Maupassant too had something to imply as well as something to state. One sees all through his work how money and passion, avarice and jealousy, physical beauty and physical suffering, are dominating influences. Humanity is mad, greedy, licentious, stupid, but beautiful ; incredibly base but incredibly exalted. Maupassant, even more than Tchehov, was struck by the terrible irony of human contradictions—contradictions which were so much an integral part of himself that he could not help hating and loving humanity with equal strength. In his attitude to women the force of these contradictions sways him first one way and then another. Women may be prostitutes but they are magnificent, as in *Boule de Suif* ; they are rich but they are also depraved; they are poor but generous; they are beautiful but mean ; they are divine but deceitful ; they may be farm-girls or lonely English virgins, as in *Miss Harriet*, but they are at once pitiable and stupid ; they have beautiful bodies but empty heads and, alas, even emptier hearts.

It has been said that Flaubert, by taking the young Maupassant in hand, ruined for ever a great popular writer. Does the statement bear examination ? I hardly think it does. Maupassant, it is true, was more prolific than his master, less an aesthete, more inventive, less detached. To him words and humanity were a kind of aphrodisiac, stimulating rapid cycles of creative passion. This tendency of his, working unchecked by others, might have resulted in a tenth-rate sex-romanticist. Fortunately it was checked by others. It was checked by the two things which combine perhaps more than any others to prevent a writer from attaining the junk status of two-penny-library popularity : remorseless clarity of vision and equally remorseless integrity of mind. Whatever else stimulated Maupassant, these forces governed him. They struck out of his finest work any possibility of fake, but equally they removed from it any possibility of moral attitude. Maupassant, of course, has been stigmatized by successive generations of the straitlaced as highly immoral. But in fact he was amoral, and that fact alone kept him from entering the most palatial spaces of popular approval and acceptance.

Maupassant and Tchehov, indeed, are alike in this : they are not part of the popular stream, " the great tedious onrush," as Mr. E. M. Forster says of history. Great though they are, they must always be, unless humanity shows some startling signs of change, part of a movement that is small if measured by the vast standard of popular demand. " There is a public," said Tchehov, " which eats salt beef and horse-radish sauce with relish, and does not care for artichokes and asparagus." To that public the flavour of *The Darling*, and in a slightly less degree *Maison Tellier*, must always remain, unfortunately, something of a mystery.

Chapter V

TOLSTOY, WELLS, AND KIPLING

THE assumption that Tchehov and Maupassant were not only the supreme but the exclusive exponents of the Russian and French short story during the nineteenth century would be unfortunate. Ruling them out, we are left with a remarkable body of writers beside whom the English writers of the corresponding period have, for the most part, the flavour of cold mutton. In Russia, Tolstoy, Turgenev, Gorki, Dostoevsky, Garshin, Andreyev, Korolenko, and in France, Flaubert, Coppée, Daudet, Anatole France, were all actively contributing to the short-story form. These names, unsupported by Tchehov and Maupassant, make their period one of the richest in the history of the short story's development. To this development no single writer in England made a contribution comparable in weight and artistry to that of Tolstoy. Having regard to the fact that in England Kipling is regarded as a national symbol standing somewhere between a stained-glass window and Nelson's monument, this statement is of course heretical. To discuss it will be part of the later purpose of this chapter. Meanwhile Tolstoy the short-story writer, disregarded for a moment as a novelist, cannot be ignored.

Tolstoy, it seems to me, exceeded with certain stories

the best standards of Tchehov and Maupassant, neither of whom wrote a more powerful story than *The Death of Ivan Ilytch*, which I have in fact heard described by a highly acute critic as the most powerful story in the world, or a more tenderly beautiful story than *Family Happiness*, which makes almost every English and American product of its time look as distinguished as the serial story in the local Friday paper. If it is compassion in Tchehov and passion in Maupassant that immediately strikes us, it is something utterly dispassionate in Tolstoy. The story of the struggle to express himself by dispassionate objectivity, to write with absolute truth, with remorseless fidelity to what his eye observed, is recorded throughout his early private diaries with constant self-criticism, dissatisfaction, and even pain. In forcing himself to carry on that struggle for supreme technical and emotional honesty in writing, Tolstoy was a revolutionary of the kind prose-writing seems to need every two generations or so. Tolstoy, like Butler and Hemingway, was, and had to be, an iconoclast. All three found the writing of their day cushioned, decorated, dusty, and dulled from ill-usage; all three beat the dull, dusty, decorated woolliness out of it, leaving it clean and spare. So that, in Tolstoy's case, Nekrasov, the editor of *The Contemporary*, wrote to him in 1855 : "Truth, in such a form as you have introduced it into our literature, is something completely new to us." [1]

Three-quarters of a century after that was written,

---

[1] Louise and Aylmer Maude : trans. *Private Diaries of Leo Tolstoy* (1853–57) (Oxford University Press)

Hemingway in *The Green Hills of Africa* is trying to define the supreme standards of prose—" prose that has never been written." It is only through the form of a dialogue that Hemingway, who shies like a nervous mare at any discussion of the harness, can bring himself to discuss the subject of literary method at all ; but finally this does emerge :

> First there must be talent, much talent. Talent such as Kipling had. Then there must be discipline. The discipline of Flaubert. Then there must be the conception of what it can be and an absolute conscience as unchanging as the standard meter in Paris, to prevent faking.

This is well said, and some such perfection of standard has been the conscious aim of many writers before Hemingway. And in 1853 Tolstoy was also saying what he felt about it :

> I am frequently held up when writing by hackneyed expressions which are not quite correct, true or poetic, but the fact that one meets them so frequently often makes me write them. These unconsidered, customary expressions, of the inadequacy of which one is aware but which one tolerates because they are so customary, will appear to posterity a proof of bad taste. To tolerate these expressions means to go with one's age, to correct them means to go in advance of it.[1]

[1] *Ibid.*, pp. 36–37. The version in the diary itself differs slightly from that quoted by Aylmer Maude in the preface. I have quoted the diary.

From the many references Tolstoy makes in these diaries to the necessity of relentless self-discipline it becomes clear that both Tolstoy and Hemingway are after the same thing. The difference is that Tolstoy has all that Hemingway demands : great talent, beside which Kipling's is that of a brass-band player, great discipline, and an " absolute conscience." Tolstoy throws further light on this, and incidentally makes a just indictment of English writing, in a later remark to his translator He speaks of the " temptation of literary allusion " and goes on, " I try to say precisely what I mean, but English-men have in their blood a desire to say things neatly rather than exactly . . . to subordinate the sense to the sound." [1]

Tolstoy's standard, inspired and shaped by a desire " to try to say precisely what I mean," is dateless ; it is the standard, however variously expressed, of all time. Its re-discovery in slightly altered form by successive generations of writers is one proof of its universality. It is the " develop, print, fix " method of Mr. Isherwood as he looks at a boarding-house in Berlin ; it is the standard to which more and more writers look, and in fact must look, as they seek to " develop, print, fix " the common history of our day.

To an inflexible honesty in trying " to say precisely what I mean " about a subject, Tolstoy added something else. It is an admirable thing to resolve " to say what I mean," but how far you are going to extend or limit the range of things you are going to talk about is another

[1] *Ibid.*

matter. A photographer may say, "I take the object exactly as I see it. No fake, no artificial background or lighting. No trickery. Absolute clarity and honesty. But mind, I only take close-ups." Thus limited, honesty of purpose and accuracy of statement may both become far easier tasks. Perfection within deliberately chosen limits is not rare, and in fact will be seen as a fairly common phenomenon in the short story of the last ten or fifteen years. The repetitive " gem of art " may have the honesty and accuracy of a statement made on oath, but repetition will sooner or later detract from even that value. Tolstoy did not make this mistake ; far from imposing limitations on himself he chose to make his range, if possible, limitless. For him it was not enough " to try to say what I mean," but to try to say it about as much of the world and humanity as possible. To limit his view of that world, to romanticize it, to set down a false impression of any part or person of it, constituted for him the cardinal sins.

Tolstoy, therefore, excels not simply in accuracy of portrayal but also in the vast range of things portrayed. As a soldier he depicted war and soldiers ; as an aristocrat he portrayed aristocrats ; but in spite of being an aristocrat he identified himself with the struggle of the serfs for emancipation : though a man of action he was attracted throughout his work towards spiritual conflict ; he was aware of what the courts call " marital incompatibility of temperament," and he portrayed that ; he was keenly aware of the beauty of the countryside and painted it in the generous, broad, accurate colours of a master ; he depicted peasants, landowners, lovers, beautiful women, cossacks, the good, bad, indifferent, happy and unhappy, faithful and unfaithful—life was never too contradictory, the range never too wide. If final perfection of portrayal sometimes eluded him, as it did in his pictures of peasants, it was not through lack of sympathy or the keen power to identify himself with the subject, but simply because the accident of class-birth robbed him of the most intimate means of contact with those outside that class, making his peasant-pictures seem, when compared with Tchehov's, as if " done with the subtle inflections of an upper-class mind." [1]

Tolstoy, indeed, was having a look at the life going on about him with a clarity of vision that seems to have had relentless sobriety. Less clouded than Tchehov's, far less fierce than Maupassant's, his eye is penetrative and dispassionate. His work gives the constant impression of great organic force. What he had to say outside his novels, in a shorter form, was not trivial ; the result had the same concentration of force, the same high finish, and was not a by-product. Tolstoy therefore belongs to that class of novelist, commoner now than in his day, who paid the short story the honour of regarding it as an equal form, not simply the recipient of what Miss Elizabeth Bowen has called " side-issues from the crowded imagination." *The Death of Ivan Ilytch, The Cossacks, Family Happiness*, and many others are great, therefore, in their own right : distinct from the novels in all ways except that of supreme distinction.

[1] Edward Garnett : *Friday Nights* (Cape)

Quite apart from his remorseless artistry in both novel and story form, Tolstoy forms an admirable introduction to the English prose fiction of his time. We have seen from some remarks of Virginia Woolf how Scott and Jane Austen, Dickens and Thackeray, Carlyle and Ruskin, the Brontës and George Eliot, Trollope and others, all lived through a great period of wars and mutinies and yet, except in two or three trivial instances, never wrote of these things. The defence of these writers might well be that these wars happened far from home, and that to describe them with factual accuracy and atmospheric truth was from a great distance an impossible task. It is true that they lacked completely the swift contact with events, the opportunities of on-the-spot reportage, now common to writers of to-day, and on that ground, perhaps, we might excuse their artistic shortcomings. But what of events at home? When we look at the state of affairs at home we find that defence collapsing.

The social and political history of Britain in the early nineteenth century, in relation to both town and country, is hardly a pretty subject. Enclosures, machine-riots, Combination Laws, Factory Acts, food riots, terrible poverty, even more terrible working conditions in factory, mill, and mine, the wholesale employment and ill-treatment of children, the truck system, the graft and cynicism of magistrates, the war of suppression on working-class rights and organizations, the scandal of jails, the appalling harshness of sentences for the most trivial crimes, the hanging of women and children, the use of armed force to intimidate and suppress the common people—all this, and much more, is recorded (if proof is needed) in the parliamentary and Home Office papers of the time. All this was history relatively as shattering and as revolutionary, as terrible and dramatic, as any of our own day. Its common theme is human suffering. In 1819, at Manchester, soldiers fired on a great assembly of people gathered to demand parliamentary reform, killing eleven persons and wounding four hundred, in the public massacre known as Peterloo ; about the same time Robert Owen gave evidence before Peel's Committee that children of six and seven, even four or five, and in some cases of three, worked fifteen hours a day in mills at a temperature of 75 to 85 degrees ; in 1813 two boys of eleven and twelve were sentenced to seven years' transportation for stealing ; a year later, for the same offence, a boy of fourteen was hanged ; records of children being sold like slaves, herded in serf-like masses from parish workhouses to mills, suffering incredible misery in mines, occur again and again in the authentic papers of the time. This infamous record of domestic history extends farther into the century than it is pleasant to contemplate. Yet if we turn to the novelists of the day is it to find that they were any more aware of this, the war at home, than they were of the war abroad ?

Excluding Dickens, Mrs. Gaskell, Charles Reade, and the author of *Alton Locke*, we are faced with the depressing answer that the great novelists of the day chose, apparently, to be blind to the more distressing part of the social life about them. The foremost Russian writers of the nineteenth century, from Turgenev to Gorki, are all animated in some degree by intellectual sincerity and a kind of warm-hearted liberalism ; they are constantly thinking in terms of the " new humanity." No similar common aspiration can be found among writers of the same period in England. Is it that they were indifferent, that their common heritage of middle-class culture excluded any extension of their sympathies outside that class ? Or is it simply that they regarded the novel, and indeed all prose-fiction, simply and solely as a form of entertainment whose reflection of life should be recognizably but not embarrassingly accurate ?

Perhaps they were right ; perhaps the novel should remain simply and solely a form of cultured entertainment, from which the clash of cruel forces, of man's inhumanity to man, and such subjects as hunger, injustice, cruelty to children, and social oppression should remain discreetly excluded ; and again perhaps not. But is the record of the pleasanter scene any more remarkable for fidelity ? To whom, for example, do we look for a picture of the early nineteenth-century English countryside ? Is there a Turgenev, even a Sarah Orne Jewett ? Again we are forced back on Mrs. Gaskell. The interpretation of nature is otherwise left to the poets, such as Wordsworth, Tennyson, Crabbe, and Clare, to scattered diarists, and above all to Cobbett ; later came Hudson and Jefferies and, among the novelists, Hardy.

These are questions we must primarily ask of the novelists, but they are applicable also to the short-story writers. Indeed there is no need to address these questions a second time, since novelists and short-story writers are here the same people. The short story has at this time no equal status with the novel ; nor has it any marked affinity with poetry ; novelists are novelists, poets are poets, and the time has not yet come when poets have been turned aside from idle lyricism by the impact of a series of world catastrophes, each of which disturbs the smooth surface of the personal world with waves of increasingly greater barbarity. Poets are still cultured men with long hair and velveteen jackets and a tendency towards nobility of thought ; prose is, generally speaking, outside their trade.

But the turn of the short story is coming, and its influence and popularity are, from 1850 onwards, spreading from America and the continent. Writers of distinction begin to understand, and then exploit, its possibilities as a separate form. Among those writers, whose collective expression may be said to have been made in *The Yellow Book* of the 'nineties, several names stand out : Stevenson, George Moore, Wilde, Wells, Kipling, and the almost forgotten Hubert Crackanthorpe. Of these Kipling is the great untouchable ; in spite of being perhaps the most execrable famous poet the language has ever produced he has become a kind of national mouthpiece ; in times of national crisis, of great wars and expectant sacrifice, the zeal with which the English quote Shakespeare is only equalled by the ardour with which they cite Kipling. Both as a poet and as a short-story writer Kipling was something of a phenomenon—

perhaps a psychological one—and as something outside the main stream of the short story's progress must be treated separately.

All the rest have a lineage well within such tradition as the short story can show. Wells is the product of a union between Dickens and Poe ; Stevenson derives from Scott and Dumas and Poe ; George Moore, whose early crude flaccidity is almost unbelievable, sat successively at the feet of Turgenev and the French ; Crackanthorpe and Wilde come from the same temples of worship. In the hands of these writers, reinforced slightly later by James, Conrad, Galsworthy, Bennett, and Maugham, the short story ceased to be the starved orphan of the earlier century and became a well-nourished and lusty infant, masculine of course, whose cries were heard round the world. Before the century closed the English short story at last showed signs of becoming something ; it emerged from a flabby anonymous embryo into something vigorous and positive. This sudden positive emergence has been partially responsible for the myth that the 'nineties were, in England at any rate, the short story's golden age. Even to-day, fifty years later, the sigh goes up (even from young writers) for the heyday of the 'nineties. For myself, I have always doubted whether that myth and that heyday would stand up to examination.

One of the strong points of the 'nineties period to which its champions always point triumphantly is its masculinity. This seems to imply that the short story, in order to be good, must always be masculine. Its movement must be bold and forceful ; its meaning must be expressed through a fluent series of physical actions ; to these actions must be added a culminating point, in which action and emotion will crystallize, leaving the reader stimulated but satisfied. In such a story femininity, passivity, introspection, the subtle and oblique, will have little or no place.

Is it true that the 'nineties short story depended for its success on these things ? Setting aside Kipling for the moment, Wells was probably its most successful exponent. On what does Wells mostly depend ? Not masculinity it is certain. Not primarily action. Wells is a scientific inventor inoculated with a dream bacillus ; he is the teller of fairy tales talking in the language of scientific power. However Wells is analysed, I think, it will be found that every characteristic of him is forcefully and diametrically opposed by something opposite. The story may be of the wildest improbability, perhaps, but its narrator, or the mind through which it is narrated, is that of the commonest earth-bound man. The story may be exceedingly subtle in complexity, but Wells's attitude is one of the greatest humility, as if to say, " This is all a bungling chap like me can make of it." The story may project a dream world, but is in reality a social criticism. It may deal with an astronomical miracle, but is related in almost liturgical terms with strong Biblical rhythms. These and other opposing forces make of Wells a powerful dynamo capable of a tireless generation of ideas scintillating with a capricious and furious fancy.

He has been well described as a sort of literary Edison, and like Edison he was born at the right time. At pretty well any preceding period of history Wells and Edison might have stood an excellent chance of being hanged. But the moment was made for Wells, and that moment has been well described by Mr. Frank Swinnerton :

> Picture to yourselves the shock to readers of those days of a rush of new inventions, simple to us now, but then so novel and startling. . . . Here was a man who put posers—scientific posers—with the facility and enjoyment of a child ; who said " Why ? " " What if—— ? " " How ? " " I suppose "—about all sorts of things people found they wanted to know. It was prodigious . . . he bubbled with new notions, and they were notions to which other minds jumped an instant too late.[1]

Poe, as I have pointed out, anticipated the nineteenth-century hunger for dream worlds and scientific fantasy, but satisfied it only partially. Wells satisfied it completely. In an age when naturalism was the most advanced of literary fashions Wells was not interested in naturalism ; in the short stories, at any rate, he was not interested in life as it was. " It is always about life being altered that I write, or about people developing schemes for altering life," he himself says. " And I have never once ' presented ' life. My apparently most objective books are criticisms and incitements to change." To

[1] Frank Swinnerton : *The Georgian Literary Scene* (Hutchinson)

this restless desire to invert life, to turn it inside out, Wells brought a kind of impishness; and it is significant that in the hands of good cartoonists he is often portrayed with something of the attitude of a small boy holding a pin behind his back. With that pin Wells caused, indeed, any amount of delicious and exciting havoc in the flat, complacent, three-dimensional world of his time. Wells was unwilling to exclude the wildest improbability about life on earth. Supposing it were ten-dimensional instead of three? Supposing men could be made invisible? Supposing a man walked through a door and disappeared? Supposing we were not the only human beings in the cosmic world? Supposing men could fly? It is first in the abundance of such ideas, rather than their startling newness, and then in his manipulation of them into credible narratives, that Wells excels. For clearly other people before Wells must have wondered if a man could suddenly disappear, or if men could fly, or if there were living creatures on other stars. For the task of making such ideas credible Wells possessed no other apparatus than that possessed by every writer in the world: words. Ideas, as most writers know, are two a penny. It is only by the translation of these ideas into words of a certain credible order that they can be given even ephemeral value for another person.

This is a truism, of course; but Wells has been derided as a stylist, as a Cockney vulgarian with " no sense of or care for beauty of style." But Wells's style has, in fact, a special kind of beauty: the beauty of artfulness.

Take *The Story of the Late Mr. Elvesham*. " I set this story down," says Wells in the opening sentence, " not expecting it will be believed." The touch is apparently that of a simple bland innocence ; in reality it is an opening of beautiful subtlety ; for it is followed at once by the very thing which Wells is anxious that the reader should swallow : " but, if possible, to prepare a way of escape for the next victim. He perhaps may profit by my misfortune. My own case, I know, is hopeless, and I am now in some measure prepared to meet my fate." The mind of the reader, abruptly stimulated, is set into eager motions of inquiry. Escape ? Victim ? Misfortune ? Hopeless ? Fate ? By these words he has been cajoled by Wells into a world of mysterious and incalculable promise. Perhaps a shade too far ? Not to be believed perhaps, after all ? But Wells holds him back from these speculations on improbability by a plain statement of the most commonplace kind of fact. " My name is George Edward Eden. I was born at Trentham, in Staffordshire, my father being employed in the gardens there."

Several points in this apparently artless business call for comment and absolve Wells from the charge of stylelessness. Two are points of fact, two are points of word-arrangement. In stating the narrator's two Christian names, George Edward, and in giving not only the place of his birth but the county, Wells gives the whole statement the authentic validity of a birth certificate. He holds it firm on earth. The two examples of word-arrangement are conceived with comparable subtlety. " I am now in some measure prepared," and " my father being employed " are both examples of the most deliberate stylelessness. For the voice here is not Wells's voice, but the voice of the narrator. This is not Wells's idea of good style but the narrator's idea of good style. It is the utterance of the common man who, making a public statement, drops his natural manner and speaks in what he feels is " proper English." It is the subtle key to character.

This artful use of apparently trivial items of fact and apparently commonplace touches of formal style is to be seen repeatedly in Wells, although it is by no means Wells's invention. Through Dickens Wells derived the technique of artful artlessness from Defoe, who used it to perfection to describe with captivating validity and realism places and events he had never seen. And in this, I think, lies much of Wells's charm as a writer—the sort of charm that will, at some future date, give Wells an attractive touch of period bloom—and almost all his power as a story-teller. For Wells possesses not only a highly compressed vitality but the great power of doing what he likes with the reader's curiosity. By coaxing it, teasing it, disturbing it, tickling it, holding it in check, shocking it, Wells succeeds in leading that curiosity to investigate the most improbable situations with a sense of anticipation and excitement. For that reason, even if someone should some day explode completely the Wells of scientific and social ideas, he will always remain a great story-teller—perhaps a great kidder would be better, a man who succeeded in telling more tall stories than any other writer of his generation and yet, by a genius for binding the commonplace to the most astronomical exploration of fancy, succeeded in getting them believed.

Wells, indeed, is a parabolist, but with a difference. For his are not earthly stories with a heavenly meaning, but heavenly stories with an earthly meaning—perhaps more accurately an earthly warning. For Wells, like a true parabolist, is also something of a prophet ; the Wellsian flights of fancy become, within Wells's own lifetime, things of momentous and terrible actuality. The dream-world in 1895 is the world of terror-reality in 1941. This is well known, of course, and I mention it only to enforce a point of contrast with Wells's greatest popular rival of the 'nineties, Kipling, born exactly one year earlier, in 1865. Wells is the prophet, the seer, the visionary who has the doubtful satisfaction of seeing his visions become all too terribly true ; he is the social iconoclast who smashes one age to pieces in order to show how another, and better, may be built and then sees a worse one building. Kipling, by contrast, is the voice of a dying hierarchy which, for all its cruelty, violence, and stupid complacency and reaction, he seeks to perpetuate.

Kipling, like Hitler, chose the swastika for an emblem, and if the two men have nothing else in common they share a love of the most extravagant form of patriotism, flamboyant stage effects and sadistic contempt for the weak ; and for those who relish the study of literature by a process of psychological analysis it is worth noting, perhaps, that as a child Kipling suffered great cruelty and distress at the hands of a nurse into whose charge his parents, on leaving India, placed him. The inversion of that cruelty finds expression again and again throughout Kipling's work, where beating and whipping are the constant media by which the problems of life are solved and its justice satisfied. An early story, *The Mark of the Beast*, in which two Anglo-Indians torture a native, is said to have revolted Andrew Lang, as well it might, and to have disgusted William Sharp, who advised its instant burning. A similar appetite for physical suffering informs *The Light that Failed*, *The Mutiny of the Mavericks*, and that story whose disgusting ending, " What was left of Bronckhorst was sent home in a carriage ; and his wife wept over it and nursed it into a man again," has become significantly famous.

In any examination of Kipling's work this fact, together with another, must be borne in mind. If Kipling, as a man, offers an interesting pathological study for those who care to make it, he must remain a profound disappointment to those who, hearing of his immense renown as a writer, expect to find in him any trace of fine quality. The notion that Kipling was a great writer is a myth. Kipling began, and remained, a journalist ; a journalist who had the luck, like Wells, to be born at the right moment in history and to have spent his childhood in the most romantic and mutinous of British overseas possessions. To describe Kipling as a journalist is not to deny him talent but to grant him, on the other hand, certain very considerable and specialized talents. These talents can best be separated and investigated by quotation.

The horror, the confusion, and the separation of the murderer from his comrades were all over before I came. There remained only on the barrack-square the blood of man calling from the ground. The hot sun had dried it to a dusky goldbeater-skin film, cracked lozenge-wise by the heat ; and as the wind rose, each lozenge, rising a little, curled up at the edges as if it were a dumb tongue. Then a heavier gust blew all away down wind in grains of dark-coloured dust.

In this short passage Kipling's qualities are well seen. The projection of the scene by a series of flamboyant images, all showy and theatrical in tone, is an excellent example of the journalistic " eye " for a dramatic and bloody moment. " Dusky goldbeater-skin film," " dumb tongues," " the blood of man calling from the ground " are all vivid, stagey, and spurious effects which are combined to create a main effect of disturbance, violence, and great tropical heat. " The blood of man " is a typical example of Kipling's use of counterfeit Biblical English, common to almost every page he wrote, and behind every line lies a certain impression of arrogance, of an aggressive mind speaking without reticence, consistently underestimating the receptive qualities of the reader. The whole is an expression of the gospel of contemptuous over-riding force which found such illuminating expression in the famous line,

" Or lesser breeds without the law." For Kipling, like Hitler, had little but contempt for the common individual —what he called " the poor brute man, an imperfectly denatured animal intermittently subject to the unpredictable reactions of an unlocated spiritual area." That contempt caused him, again like Hitler, to separate mankind into classes, regardless of character. The elect were strong, arrogant men of swift high action. And the rest ? For all Kipling cared they might be one with the nigger that " you treat . . . to a dose of cleanin' rod."

This authoritarian attitude, colouring Kipling's style throughout, creates the impression that Kipling does not consider himself by any means on equal terms with the reader. The reader is being told, and must listen. Nor is the projection of a highly coloured scene enough ; Kipling, anxious to assist and if necessary beat the reader into accepting some point, conclusion, or philosophy of his own, seldom permits him to do the final thinking. Again and again the moral—often in that pseudo-Biblical English that is one of the inseparable attributes of cheap journalism — is clapped on to the end of the story. "Member of more learned and scientific societies," ends The Miracle of Phanda Bhagat, " than will ever do any good in this world or the next"—a conclusion at once arrogant and cheap, a private conclusion, part of Kipling's personal autocracy, forced on the reader regardless of whether he wants it or not.

The spurious Biblical lilt in Kipling offers a moment of interesting study. It is to be noted that the two best-selling novelists of his day, beside whom Wells lived on bread and cheese, were Marie Corelli and Hall Caine, who hoodwinked an enormous public by the use of the same trick. That trick consisted simply of wrapping up melodramatic sexual scandal in a highly moral atmosphere and telling the resultant story in prose subtly flavoured by the rhythm of the one book which, to millions of Victorian readers, was the indisputable " word." Kipling had little to say of sexual scandal, but he had a great deal to say of a species of civilized barbarism, the suppression of the weak and the grinding down of coloured illiterates in the cause of Empire, which if it had been painted realistically must have made Kipling the outcast of his time. Kipling, by the use of a very highly coloured method of reporting, purported to paint it realistically but in reality painted it from an attitude so biased by blood, creed, and class that it is almost mystical. The moral pseudo-Biblical tone enabled him to make palatable both episodes and the creeds inspiring them, when otherwise they would have been wholly disgusting. As Mr. Hugh Kingsmill has pointed out : " Kipling's England was the England of the Athenaeum, Carlton and Beefsteak Clubs, of the country-house, and *the working population as it shows itself to the well-to-do.*" [1]

The italics are mine. There was no other point of view. Kipling's Tom Atkins is, in consequence, as real as a ventriloquist's doll, though his attempt to portray soldiers seems generally to have been both realistic and sincere. His natives are voiceless ; they have no say in

[1] Hugh Kingsmill : *Rudyard Kipling* (Horizon, Vol. II., No. 9)

the government of this world. Yet, as Kipling well knew, they *had* a voice, though it spoke another language ; and a greater man could have interpreted it. But Kipling chose to interpret only one voice—the voice of the ruling caste speaking, as Mr. Kingsmill says, in " clipped speech and mannered stoicism," and of designs and creeds made to seem more " right," more " glorious," and more " heaven-blessed " when explained in the soothing rhythm of God's own book.

As with Wagner, there are no two ways about Kipling. Either the loud and brassy twilights, with their romantic gods, are something incomparably wonderful, or they are something of incomparably false vulgarity. Here, in fact, it may not be irrelevant to recall two opinions of Wagner—that of Hitler, who declared, " At any stage of my life I came back to him " ; and that of Sibelius, who said, " Wagner is rude, brutal, vulgar, completely lacking in delicacy." So with Kipling. On the one side stand the classes and societies who still reverence his creed of Empire, dead though it has long been, and quote him with scriptural solemnity in times of crisis and war ; on the other hand stand the heretics, among whom I am inevitably numbered, to whom no single syllable of Kipling has ever given a moment's pleasure. He is a writer who arouses, just as he depicts, violent emotions, but I should be surprised if there were any quality of affection among them. I have tried to show how, talented though he was, he is unacceptable as a stylist. To explain his failure as a man would, without some process of psychological analysis, be far more difficult. Yet the character of the man, as of all other writers, seeps through and is implicit in the work. In that implied *persona* I see none of the attributes which, for me, are part of the character of the greatest writers. There is no all-embracing tolerance, as in Tchehov ; no attempt, as in Maupassant, to paint all types with the same ruthless detachment and objectivity ; no benevolence ; no good-hearted friendliness, even, as in Hardy ; no impression of fatalism and nobility, as in Conrad ; no sublime and generous acceptance and understanding of every class and type as seen in Dickens and Shakespeare; none of Wells's iconoclasm, no liberalism, none of that Russian "pureness of soul." One gets instead the impression of a writer whose outlook is one of harsh, confused, egotistical mysticism, of a voice vulgar and cruel in its class intolerance. As time goes on we shall see better whether Kipling's picture of India is right. For now, fifty years after Kipling's autocratic heyday (note that he seldom appeared in anthologies and that for years he approved no cheap edition of his works), the emancipated native writers of India are at last beginning to speak of their own country. The voice which Kipling chose not to hear is now speaking for itself with a quality of realistic and poetic truth that will throw an interesting light on Kipling's tinsel and brass.

Turning from Wells and Kipling to the general scene of late nineteenth-century short-story writing, is to be struck by an interesting fact. There is no collective trend ; writers are allied in no movement. All, it is true, are occupied by the production of stories which are examples of active rather than passive types of narration. (This is for the moment to except James, who is something of an English-American hybrid.) A certain similarity of method can be observed in Stevenson, Doyle, and Wells, but this is the result and not the cause of a trend. It is the late fruit of Poe. Of Stevenson it would be enough, perhaps, to recall George Moore's sally—quite as precious as the object of its criticism, " I think of Mr. Stevenson as a consumptive youth wearing garlands of sad flowers with pale weak hands, or leaning to a large plate-glass window, and scratching thereon exquisite profiles with a diamond pencil "—if it were not for some excellent pieces of realistic excitement such as *Markheim*, *Thrawn Janet*, or *Dr. Jekyll and Mr. Hyde*. In Doyle may be seen another expression of Wells's method—fancy tied hard to earth by circumstantial detail, horror made plausible by being projected against the everyday scene, the improbable and eccentric detective set off by the ordinary, humdrum doctor, symbol of the puzzled and good-natured reader.

No one of this class, except Wells, is going anywhere. If we look at their contemporaries we shall see the same evidence of derivation. Gissing is a minor echo of Dickens ; Wilde is a product of Hans Andersen who has been impeccably laundered *en route* by the French naturalists ; Hubert Crackanthorpe is interesting only as an attempt to transplant Maupassant on English soil. A sifting of Mr. Heinemann's list of 1895 fails to produce from the spangled ladies and gentlemen of the time— Hall Caine, Sarah Grand, Flora Annie Steele, Ouida,

Zangwill, Maxwell Gray, W. J. Locke, etc.—more than one other short-story writer of distinction, who unfortunately became too notorious in other respects for a proper appreciation of his talent. Frank Harris, in such volumes as *The Yellow Ticket* and *Elder Conklin*, produced stories of straight naturalism which still read excellently to-day. With the exception of H. H. Munro (Saki), who can be seen in a more proper perspective with the Leacock - Thurber - Wodehouse school of humour, and George Moore, who was still wrestling with the problem—unusual for an Irish writer—of trying to write English fluently, there are no other names of distinction until the turn of the century. Moore's *The Untilled Field* did not appear until 1902, and Conrad's reputation was not made till some years later.

The whole carefully bolstered structure of the 'nineties period of short-story greatness will be seen to rest, therefore, on less than a dozen important names, of which only half can file a claim for consideration in the first class.

But as the century turns something interesting and important is happening. The short story, it is worth noting, has not yet attracted, in England, any woman writer of importance. But for the next thirty or forty years, from the 'nineties onwards, the most important influence on the English short story is to be the work of a woman. In a stone cottage on the Surrey hills, towards the close of the century, a little wiry woman of the greatest personal charm and sensibility gently tempered with Scots caution, began a series of translations from the Russian which, in bulk alone, constitute a superhuman achievement. Without Constance Garnett's genius and astonishing industry in translating Turgenev, Tolstoy, Gogol, Dostoevsky, Gorki, and Tchehov, the history of twentieth-century English literature, notably that of the short story and the drama, must inevitably have been a very different thing. How the short story would have developed, uninfluenced by these translations, not only in England but in America, it is impossible to divine. It might have been better or it might have been worse : it must have been different. Uninfluenced by the translations of Tchehov, Katherine Mansfield could hardly, in spite of Mr. Murry's denials, have written as she did, and the English short story might never have been wrested from the grasp of writers who worked as it were in a corner, confining the short story to the narrow limits of fantasy. The short story might have remained unexplorative, and so in a sense undemocratic, a thing of unexpanded sympathies, never breaking out into the open air of ordinary life from its box of matchwood artificiality. It is certain that the short story would finally have emerged somehow—but how, we can only speculate. So it is undeniable, I think, that between the turn of the century and the end of the Great War the most important literary events exercising an outside influence on the English and American short story were the Garnett translations, first of Turgenev, then of Tchehov. That this was only one of many events working together for the post-war emancipation of the short story is equally true. For the emergence of the short story was hastened by a social revolution, just as that revolution was inconceivably hastened by war. After 1914 writers of all kinds, but especially older writers who had achieved stability before that time, were to be " confounded by the pressure exerted upon their sensibilities, first by the war, later by the peace." [1] But there were others who had achieved no stability. They saw no escape in mechanical structure and consequent financial freedom in prosperous magazines. There were still others, very young, who had, as it were, cut their teeth on the army rifles left carelessly about in the corners of the home, and who should have been poets. And among these are the short-story writers of to-day.

[1] E. J. O'Brien : intro., *Best Short Stories, 1927* : *English*

CHAPTER VI

KATHERINE MANSFIELD AND
A. E. COPPARD

As the aftermath of one war resolved itself into the transitional period of preparation for another we were promised a renaissance in literature. After periods of national suffering, sacrifice, and victory, we were assured, the literature of a nation, fed on blood and glory, is seen to emerge with more virile splendour. Now, we heard, there will begin a notable period of poetry and drama, but most notably of poetry.

This renaissance, for reasons not hard to find, failed lamentably to mature. In the first place the sort of renaissance visualized was that in which the symbols of honour and glory would be the theme of songs sung on a major note ; something was anticipated, I think, that would combine the martial patriotism of Kipling with that of the speech before Agincourt. In the second place, and most unfortunately, many poets could no longer sing, for the simple reason that they had been blown to bits. Those of their poet-comrades who did return saw before them a future of arid futility, for which there could be no expression in a major key and possibly no expression at all. It is not surprising, therefore, that the most popular poets of the immediate post-war period were Brooke, Noyes, Masefield, Drinkwater, and Housman, of whom only the last has any claim to be regarded as anything but a minor figure. The poetic renaissance was in fact a fiasco, just as the drama renaissance, if you cut out Shaw and O'Casey, was also a fiasco. The youngest generation of all, out of which the new poets were supposedly to emerge, found itself with voices that had broken too early, and heads that were old before their time. What they had to say was too much the sour fruit of frustration to find expression in lyricism, and yet was too urgent to be wrapped up in the complacent folds of ordinary prose. That generation (the number of notable English and American short-story writers born between 1900 and 1910 will be found to be an interesting figure) needed and sought as a form something between lyric poetry and fictional prose. That form it found, and proceeded to develop as its own, in the short story.

It may be a coincidence, but if so it is an interesting coincidence, that immediately the Great War was over two important writers found their natural expression, as prose writers, solely and exclusively in the short story— an event for which there was no important English precedent except Kipling. I do not suppose these writers thought of themselves as innovators setting a fashion. Nevertheless their action in choosing the short story as a medium was the beginning of a fashion, if you can call it that, which in the next twenty years was to attract the following of scores of young writers for whom expression through poetry was not enough. Indeed it is

not too much to say, I think, that Katherine Mansfield
and A. E. Coppard, for all their faults and their debt to
Tchehov, succeeded more than any other writers of
their day in assisting the English short story to a state of
adult emancipation. Before their time the short story
in English had known imagination, as in Poe, ingenuity,
as in Wells, masculinity, as in Kipling, humour and
trickery, as in O. Henry, colour and irony, as in Crane,
together with most of the virtues and vices of the novel ;
but with the possible exception of Conrad, himself only
just coming into his own, it had been very little touched
by poetry. Lyricism was kept outside it ; poets, having
their own medium, left it alone. But it will remain
eternally to the credit of Katherine Mansfield and A. E.
Coppard that both attempted to bring to the short story
some of the fancy, delicacy, shape, and coloured conceit
of the Elizabethan lyric—a comparison especially true
in the case of Coppard—and that when they left it the
short story had gained new vitality and new design and
above all, perhaps, a certain quality of transparency.

To carry the comparison of these two writers any
further would, I think, be unprofitable. Yet we may
remark, before dealing with them separately, that both
are the meeting-places of Russian and English influences
—Katherine Mansfield combining Tchehov and Virginia
Woolf (by way, perhaps, of Dorothy Richardson),
Coppard combining Tchehov and, rather surprisingly,
Henry James. Both had the satisfaction of being
acclaimed, in the early twenties, as highly original
writers—yet it would be truer to say, I think, that both

were more remarkable as the means of transmitting certain influences than originating them. Neither disrupted, as Joyce did, the prose of their time ; neither excited the moral and mystical controversies of *Ulysses* and *The Rainbow* ; neither shook the foundations of society, like Samuel Butler. Yet after them, as after Joyce, Lawrence, and Butler, the things they touched could never be quite the same again.

Katherine Mansfield was born in New Zealand in 1888 ; she was writing, very immaturely and unsuccessfully, as early as 1909, that is when she was twenty-one. Between that date and the end of the Great War she wrote a certain number of stories, some of which were collected in a still-born volume, *In a German Pension*, in 1911. But it is not until 1917, after the profound spiritual shock of war and her younger brother's death, that " her mind began to turn back towards her early childhood as a life which had existed apart from, and uncontaminated by, the mechanical civilization which had produced the war." [1] In that same year, and as a result of that reorientation, she produced her first story of importance, originally called *The Aloe*, a charming title which for some reason she changed to *Prelude*. This story, appearing separately as a paper-bound volume, fell utterly flat, and was noticed by only two papers. In 1920 appeared her second volume, *Bliss*, for which she received the dizzy sum of £40 in advance, and in 1922, when she was extremely ill and in fact almost dying, appeared the

[1] J. Middleton Murry : intro. *Letters of Katherine Mansfield, 1914–22* (Constable)

volume which established her reputation beyond any doubt—*The Garden Party*.

From these few facts some interesting conclusions emerge. Her writing life covered a period of roughly ten years ; her output, in spite of the loyal but sometimes tiresome efforts of Mr. Middleton Murry to sift her waste-paper basket, is quite small ; during the writing of most of this work she was in a rarefied state of spiritual and physical suffering, an invalid desperately working out her own personal destiny, of which her stories are an undetached part; lastly, and largely as the result of the fact that that personal destiny was never fully resolved, only a fraction of her work can be regarded as mature. Like Keats, whose measure of sensuous sensibility her own so closely resembles, she will be the subject of generations of literary speculators, who will wonder what she might have done if she could only have lived on.

What, then, is the secret of her achievement ? What did she do ? Why is her achievement influential ?

The answer is primarily simple. Her art, and her particular application of it to the short story, was intensely personal. She is a writer with a flavour. Just as D. H. Lawrence can be detected as the central figure of most of his work, so Katherine Mansfield is the unseen and unspeaking personality behind every page she wrote. From her letters she will be seen as a personality capable of spontaneous but unenduring responses ; her mind is quick, nervous, in a state of constant receptive flutter ; her eye takes in the imagery of surrounding life in a

series of wonderfully vivid and excited impressions ; all
these receptions and responses are, in the first place,
emotional, only secondarily to be analysed, if at all,
at some later moment of personal catechism and distrust.
All this is heightened and aggravated by the complaint
from which she suffered—so that she is either very much
up or very much down. Such a state of personal tension,
alternately exultant and despondent, inevitably shapes and
colours her work ; but behind it lies a strong force of
personal courage, finding its expression in a gaiety that
is exuberant, slightly ironical, and sometimes quite school-
girlish in its eagerness to demonstrate how she can
triumph over suffering.

All this is the woman emotionally shaping the writer.
This is the secret, the genius if you care to put it so, that
cannot be copied. But a state of consumptive emotional
tension cannot, of itself, shape short stories, and it would
be surprising if so receptive a personality as Katherine
Mansfield's were to have been wholly uninfluenced by
other practitioners.

Katherine Mansfield read widely, and was in fact so
influenced. The key influence to her work has always
been regarded as Tchehov. This Mr. Middleton Murry,
rather hastily I think, denies :

There is a certain resemblance between Katherine
Mansfield's stories and those of Anton Tchehov. But
this resemblance is often exaggerated by critics, who
seem to believe that Katherine Mansfield learned her
art from Tchehov. That is a singularly superficial

view of the relation, which was one of kindred temperaments. In fact Katherine Mansfield's technique is very different from Tchehov's. She admired and understood Tchehov's work as few English writers have done ; she had (as her *Journal* shows) a deep personal affection for the man, whom, of course, she never knew. But her method was wholly her own, and her development would have been precisely the same had Tchehov never existed.[1]

Two remarks in this defence call for some comment. To say that Tchehov and Katherine Mansfield were " kindred temperaments " is, it seems to me, a slightly rash statement from a man who knew one person with great and therefore biased intimacy and the other not at all. Again, the categorical statement that " her development would have been precisely the same had Tchehov never existed " seems to me to belong to the realm of highly problematical prophecy. No one, not even Mr. Middleton Murry, should confuse criticism with clairvoyance. And since there is nothing sinister in Tchehov's influence, but in fact something wholly good for a writer of Katherine Mansfield's temperament, there can be no harm in facing the fact that she learned, and was probably delighted to learn, from someone who was a master of the form she loved.

From Tchehov, it seems to me, Katherine Mansfield learned, or had her attention drawn to, two important

[1] J. Middleton Murry : intro. *Letters of Katherine Mansfield, 1914–22* (Constable)

things that had hitherto found no place in the English
short story : casual and oblique narration. Like Tchehov,
Katherine Mansfield saw the possibilities of telling the
story by what was left out as much as by what was left
in, or alternately of describing one set of events and
consequences while really indicating another. Her
shades of tone and meaning are subtle ; but they differ
from Tchehov's in one important thing. Tchehov's
stories have a certain greyness of tone—he works in
pencil and pastel. Katherine Mansfield's are vivid and
clearly coloured—the light shines through them as it
shines through a picture of stained glass. That side of
her art, though enriched primarily by her remarkable
natural gifts of observation, has much in common with
the art of two of her contemporaries, Virginia Woolf and
Miss Dorothy Richardson. Like theirs also, her art is
essentially feminine ; she delights in making her characters show their thoughts by a kind of mental soliloquy,
fluttering, gossipy, breathless with question and answer:
" What did garden parties and baskets and lace-
frocks matter to him ? He was far from all these things.
He was wonderful, beautiful. While they were laughing
and while the band was playing, this marvel had come
to the lane. Happy . . . Happy . . . All is well, said
that sleeping face. This is just as it should be. I am
content." [1] Or again, and this time from a story for
which a close parallel may be found in Tchehov too :
" Was it—could it all be true ? It sounded terribly true.
Was this first ball only the beginning of her last ball after

[1] *The Garden Party* (Constable)

all ? At that the music seemed to change ; it sounded sad, sad ; it rose upon a great sigh. Oh ! how quickly things changed ! Why didn't happiness last for ever ? For ever wasn't a bit too long." [1] Here question and answer keep the surface of the style in constant ebb and flow ; the rhetoric is delicate and rippling ; it reads easily ; one skims over the surface.

But the dangers of such a style are clear. There is the danger that the voice of the narrator may become confused, even though wrongly, with the voice of the character ; and one feels in certain of Katherine Mansfield's stories that this has happened, and that the girlish, chattering voice is the voice of the writer thinly disguised. Then there is the danger of monotony—of becoming bored, as one does in life, by a voice talking constantly of itself and answering all its own questions before anyone else has a chance. Lastly, as the method is repeated, it tends to give even very different characters a touch of sameness, until they are all chattering overgrown schoolgirls busy asking and answering breathless facile questions about love and life and happiness.

Character indeed, that is, the building up of character, was not Katherine Mansfield's strong point. She catches at people—very ordinary, very lonely, very happy, very pathetic people—as they pass ; she succeeds in extracting from each, as it were, a moment or two of self-revelation, gives them her blessing and lets them slip through her kindly, sympathetic fingers. They pass into the mist of crowds and remain there : interesting

[1] *Her First Ball* (Constable)

memories which gradually fade as the reader's sense of pity for them fades, until they become negative and remote again. It is here in fact that the popular comparison with Tchehov must begin to break down— for where in Tchehov we both feel and know more about a character as it steps beyond the story than we did in the beginning, in Katherine Mansfield we have an impression only of feeling, and not of knowing, more. It is our hearts that have been the object of attack. Tchehov's characters, for all their pencil greyness of tone, step beyond the boundaries of his stories firmly as characters, forming in their immense variation a whole Russian national portrait gallery. Katherine Mansfield, catching at a couple of dozen types, these mostly young girls and women, can nowhere challenge the greatness of Tchehov's range. Her art in fact lacked—because she was ill, because her personality was never fully resolved, because she died young—the Russian's final objective strength. Time and circumstance limited its development, leaving it supremely personal, as it were soft-boned, with a certain rosy delicacy, but in all final tests of comparison immature.

Yet Katherine Mansfield became known and talked of, in the nineteen-twenties and perhaps even in the early 'thirties, as the greatest of all new influences on the short story. Many good writers of stories were writing at about that time, among them Maugham, Galsworthy, Conrad, and George Moore, to say nothing of the person who wrote that supreme but unwanted volume, *Dubliners*, and their work has so far stood the time-test as well as, in some cases much better than, her own. Why did she put the short-story world into a flutter? Was it because, almost for the first time, the English short story stopped being concerned with set situations, improbabilities, facile action, artificial dilemmas? It has been recorded that the printer of *Prelude* exclaimed, " My ! but these kids are *real* ! " Was this the reason ?—that someone had at last shown that ordinary lives, unmanipulated into highly dramatic emotional entanglements, could be interesting? She turned away from much of contemporary literature for an illuminating reason—it lacked both truth, her own " devouring passion," and humility. Somewhere here, I think, in the freshness of her approach to life and in the freshness of her casual, apparently scrappy, vivid and beautifully coloured method, may be found the reason for her popular and influential success.

At her instigation, indeed, the short story suddenly turned round, as it were, and had a look at life—not Life with a capital letter, but the very ordinary yet very extraordinary life going on in suburban homes, poor streets, villages, back bedrooms, barbers' shops, cafés, hotels, in every place. The war had not only struck down the social barriers everywhere, but it had struck down the social barriers for writers especially. Katherine Mansfield stands at the beginning, though she is by no means responsible for it, of a new era of democratic literature, in which the short story was to find an exceptionally happy place. This great interest in common lives had already been fostered by Wells, in his straight fiction, and Bennett, in such work as *Clayhanger*. But after the war both Wells and Bennett were slipping out of the stream of influence, Wells into sociological fiction, Bennett into Babylonian hotels, and it was now the disruptive influence of Joyce, D. H. Lawrence, Virginia Woolf, and what has been called "the tyranny of sex" that together constituted fiction's most compelling influences. Writers, after the Great War of 1914–18, found themselves less fettered than at any time in history. They had suddenly a free pass to say and see and do and describe anything they wanted. No subject was now barred to a writer, to the last limit of physical experience.

To the short-story writer, therefore, perhaps even more than to the novelist, a world of immense new possibilities was opened up. Katherine Mansfield, showing that by freshness of approach even the most trivial aspect or incident could become vitally interesting, has her share in the opening up of that world. Her importance lies less perhaps in what she did than in the fact that she indicated what could be done. Few writers have successfully imitated her extremely personal method ; many have followed her example in squeezing the significance out of the apparently commonplace, trivial behaviour of their fellow-men.

The same touch of fancy and poetry that lifts her work out of the ordinary is found, though much more emphatically, in the stories of A. E. Coppard, who sprang suddenly into prominence in the years when *The Garden Party* was a vogue. Coppard, born in 1878, is reputed to share with Sherwood Anderson the legend of having had "a trunkful of fiction" waiting to be published when his first volumes of stories began to be issued by a private press. Certainly Coppard, who had spent some years of his life in business, had waited rather longer than most writers before opening up the literary shop. It is not surprising, therefore, that the first contents of that window should have had a certain maturity of finish that the gawky early work of Katherine Mansfield lacks. Coppard's first window display, in fact, was like a show of well-made, bright-coloured handicraft : strong in texture, bold and fanciful in design, carefully finished, fashioned from excellent native materials which, like oak and wool, had their own sweet earthy and enduring flavour. For Coppard, like Sherwood Anderson, had recognized the beauty and value of indigenous materials.

Coppard's work is contained, except for a little verse, in a dozen volumes of stories. Of these only the first six or seven are outstanding ; the work between *Adam and Eve and Pinch Me* and *Silver Circus* contains the cream of Coppard. In each of these volumes there meet a number of conflicting elements which are both the actual and the theoretical essentials of all Coppard's work : on the one hand realism, vivid factual description, earthiness, a home-brewed strength and simplicity ; on the other hand fantasy, fairy-tale impossibility, exoticism, psychological trickery and hypothesis, sophistication ; on the one hand buffoonery, punning, heartiness, bawdiness, good rounds of belly-laughter and low comedy ; on the other hand a certain literary dandiness, pretty play of words, elaborate metaphorical crochet-work, a love of subtle conceits for their own sake. As time goes on the elements of the first group are forced into secondary place by the elements of the other ; the home-brewed earthy simplicity is ousted by a kind of twilit fantasy ; the trick of telling a tale rather than of writing a story reaches a stage where it is all too patently the result of a carefully elaborated theory.

For this too must be noted about the work of Coppard : his pieces are not stories but, as he is very careful to emphasize on every fly-leaf, tales. Behind this lies Coppard's theory that the art of telling stories, since it originates by the primitive camp-fires of unread peoples far back in time, is an oral and not a written one. In elaboration of this theory he would like to see tales once more told as if in the market-place, in the inn, at the street corner (as of course they are still told) with all the asides and insertions of common wit, buffoonery, bawdiness, and comment that accompany the spoken tale everywhere. Unhappily such a theory, worked out to a logical conclusion, would mean the end of writers, who would presumably only learn their tales by heart and recite them on suitable occasions to selected audiences. Such a method of tale-telling, having much in common with folk-lore, local legend, and the spoken parable (note that Coppard delights in allegory), would depend for its effect largely on pictorial simplicity, the use of homely metaphor, and the entire absence of literary language.

Unfortunately for Coppard's theory his work shows the strongest signs—increasing rather than decreasing as time goes on—that he is in reality a very literary writer, influenced in turn by other very literary writers, notably Henry James. Throughout Coppard's work may be observed, in fact, the consequences of a strange battle between tale-telling at its simplest and tale-telling at its most sophisticated. And in this battle Henry James is the major—and regrettably I think—the winning combatant.

This corruption of Coppard's work by sophisticated influences seriously detracts from what originally promised to be a very stout, yeoman achievement, very much of the English earth, closely akin to the lyric poetry of the Elizabethans. As Coppard began speaking, in the early twenties, through such volumes as *Clorinda Walks in Heaven*, *The Black Dog*, and *Fishmonger's Fiddle*, it was clear that a poet had taken up the short story, choosing as his backgrounds the countryside of middle England, the pubs, the provincial towns with their faded breweries and gloomy old-fashioned lawyers' offices, even the East End of London and the shops of tailors' pressers. A man with ripe powers of description, an uncanny knack of weaving a tale, a keen eye for lyrical colour, a sense of both humour and tragedy, Coppard had both strong and delicate gifts. The results excited attention, as they were bound to do, for Coppard's way was refreshing and the English short story had never known such pieces as *Dusky Ruth*, *The Poor Man*, *The Higgler*, *Fishmonger's Fiddle*—stories as sturdy and sound in grain as oak, as delicate and oddly scented as hawthorn. Coppard's peculiar achievement in such stories was never subsequently surpassed. They had a flavour for which no one discovered a word until Mr. A. J. J. Ratcliff admirably described it as a " flavour of nutmeg."

But even so early as *Adam and Eve and Pinch Me*, Coppard may be seen succumbing to certain dangerous temptations. Quotations will best illustrate them :

In the main street amongst tall establishments of mart and worship was a high narrow house. (*Arabesque : The Mouse*)

But his fickle intelligence received a sharp admonitory nudge. (*The Quiet Woman*)

He was of years calendared in unreflecting minds as tender years. (*Communion*)

They were like two negative atoms swinging in a medium from which the positive flux was withdrawn. (*Craven Arms*)

The gas-tube in the violence of its disappointment contracted itself abruptly, assumed a lateral bend, and put out its tongue of flame. (*Fifty Pounds*)

All these are casually selected examples of a style of writing which Coppard never learned was bad and consequently never learned to correct. The first three are examples of provincial journalese at its best, or worst, whichever you prefer ; the fourth is a piece of pretentious word-play imposed on the main body of the story and meaning little or nothing ; the metaphor of the gas-tube is atrocious.

Yet Coppard could also write :

In front of them lay the field they had crossed, a sour scent rising faintly from its yellow blooms that quivered in the wind.   (*The Field of Mustard*)

He watched her go heavily down the stairs before he shut the door.   Returning to the bed he lifted the quilt.   The dead body was naked and smelt of soap. Dropping the quilt he lifted the outstretched arm again, like cold wax to the touch and unpliant as a sturdy sapling, and tried once more to bend it to the body's side.   As he did so the bedroom door blew open with a crash.   (*The Higgler*)

The piazza was planted with palm trees, their trunks like vast pineapples, loaded with light saffron trusses—as large as wheat sheaves—of dates.

It seems incredible that the man who wrote the first group of sentences, each so unfitted to the essential structure of the short story, should also have written the second, in which every word is admirably distilled.   Yet Coppard wrote with great care, piecing his stories together rather than writing them, noting down metaphors as they flashed on him, storing up oddities of description, odd names, odd situations, until a suitable niche was found for them in the final framework of the tale.   All this gives his work the effect, at times, of being the product of an arts-and-crafts shop.   Its apparent boisterous spontaneity is in reality studied ; the shop window with its homespun cloth and rough carving has been set out by a West End hand. Coppard cannot escape, I think, the charge of pretentiousness even in some of his best work—yet that work, as seen in *The Higgler*, *Dusky Ruth*, *Fine Feathers*, *The Cherry Tree*, *The Field of Mustard*, is as English and as sturdily beautiful as the Cotswold Hills and the Buckinghamshire beech-woods that are so often the background of Coppard's tales. On these achievements, and a dozen or so like them, Coppard's reputation may safely rest. The worst of his work can never detract from their craftsmanship or their very English beauty.

Unlike Wells and Kipling, Coppard had no sociological axes to grind. He was interested only in the tale for the tale's sake ; in his stories there is no social, religious, scientific, or imperialistic background or bias. Coppard was interested in what happened to people once they got on to the merry-go-round of emotion, and indeed his stories, half-real, half-fantastic, have something of the atmosphere of the fair-ground ; behind the well-lit exteriors lurks a certain air of gipsyish fancy and romance, and it is interesting to note that Coppard for some years chose just that gipsyish mode of life, living as he did in an isolated caravan in the Buckinghamshire woods and writing many of his best stories there.

But Coppard, forty when the Great War ended, hardly belongs to the generation of writers that cut its teeth on bullets and found the future beyond 1920 a very sadly disrupted prospect. Coppard, though always regarded

as a writer young in spirit, belongs essentially to the
generation of Conrad and Maugham. His significance
to the new generation lay in the fact that he alone of
his generation sought his expression solely in the short
story; Conrad chose as his primary medium the novel,
Maugham the play and the novel; both, though
excellent craftsmen in the shorter form, used it only as
a supplementary and not exclusive means of expression.
To young writers—and here I can speak very much
from personal experience—the choice made by Coppard
was an inspiration. To see the short story lifted from its
place as an orphan of literature, handled at last as if it
were an adult, and finally presented as a beautiful thing,
strong in its own right, gave at least one very young
writer of the 1920's great hope and encouragement, and
I have no doubt it similarly affected others.

In the early 1920's, then, largely by the inspiration of
Coppard and Katherine Mansfield, but also under the
impetus of the popularity of Conrad, Maugham, and
Galsworthy (Galsworthy's *Caravan* was the first, or
almost the first, collected " omnibus " volume of short
stories), and also of Wells and James, the short story was
ready for a new phase of development. That development was later to receive a great impetus from Ireland and
America, but in the early 'twenties the American short
story had not yet emerged from its own lean time.
" These were the years [1915–22] of the greatest com-
placence," says Mr. E. J. O'Brien. " They were the most
triumphant years of the machine. The machine and the
story-writer were both over-producing cheap standard-

ized goods. It was a boom period." [1] Writers in England were therefore not yet looking to America ; rather were writers in America—to the detriment of the period—looking to us. And they looked, if they were short-story writers, mostly to Conrad and Maugham.

By the early twenties Conrad had emerged from being a writer of successive *succès d'estime* to being a writer of literary popularity ; Maugham, too, was at the beginning of a new phase of public attention. For Maugham had begun, like George Moore, as a man quite ungifted with either a natural eye or a natural ear for style, had gone on to develop a style, and had at last become something of an ascetic in the business. Maugham indeed has had the unusual experience of making two separate reputations : a popular and fashionable reputation, built on the plays and novels, followed by a highbrow reputation, built largely on the better stories and *Cakes and Ale.*

Maugham indeed might be called a commercial artist. Not so Conrad. Nor do I think Conrad, for all the beauty and grandeur of his work, is part of the main lineage of the short story. Conrad wrote relatively few stories, of which only a fraction were really short. As a writer gifted with splendid garrulity, much influenced by Henry James, Conrad lacked the art of compression vital to expression in a very brief space. As a result his stories, of which *Heart of Darkness, The End of the Tether* and *Gaspar Ruiz* are excellent examples, belong to that controversial genre known variously as the long short story, the novelette, the *conte*, and the *novella*. In these

[1] E. J. O'Brien : intro. *Best Short Stories of 1932* (Cape)

splendid, moody, highly atmospheric and sardonically romantic stories Conrad is employing methods differing little from the methods of his novels ; he is dealing, as always, with men isolated from their fellows by ironic circumstances and presented in dramatic clashes against elemental forces. Such themes are big, calling for the spacious methods at which Conrad excelled. Their effect depended largely on the grandeur of Conrad's elaboration, on the almost oriental splendour of the language, on the subtlety of the psychological explorations. For all these the very short story, of two thousand or three thousand words, is the wrong medium, and Conrad never chose it. Three or four of his stories, as compared with a dozen or twenty of Maupassant's, were enough to make up a volume. Highly individual, aristocratic, of foreign and rather lavish temperament, Conrad stands outside the main English short story rather as he stands, isolated as its only important writer of sea stories, outside the main stream of the English novel. To the young writers of post-war England he had little to offer.

Nor, rather surprisingly, had Maugham. Maugham is at once an attractive and a rather disconcerting figure. Beginning as a writer with, as it were, no ear for words, Maugham had very early to choose a stylistic model which his own limitations would permit him to follow without embarrassment. To have chosen a pretentious, poetical, highly coloured writer would have been fatal. Maugham chose Maupassant, and throughout his career has stuck to Maupassant. It is interesting to recall here that Maupassant has been described as " the born popular writer, battered by Flaubert into austerity," and perhaps Maugham is an example of the sort of writer, popular, cosmopolitan, commercial and yet in some way distinguished, that Maupassant might have been if left alone. Maugham is now, at his best, as in *Cakes and Ale*, a master of cultivated acidity. The spare sere detachment of his prose may, with the exception of recurrent lapses into appalling sentimentality, be safely offered as a sound foundation course in commercial-literary craftsmanship.

One other influence, not I believe admitted by Maugham, seems to have shaped his craft. Repeatedly throughout his work, speaking both for himself and through his characters, Maugham reveals an ironic impatience with the stuffiness of literary and moral conventions (see the delicious dissection of the pompous social-climbing novelist in *Cakes and Ale*), and is constantly administering the acid corrective. The parallel for this side of Maugham's method is not Maupassant, but *The Way of All Flesh*, a book for which Maugham is admirably fitted to write a modern counterpart. Here are two quotations :

Like other rich men at the beginning of this century he ate and drank a good deal more than was enough to keep him in health. Even his excellent constitution was not proof against a prolonged course of overfeeding and what we should now consider overdrinking. His liver would not unfrequently get out of order, and he would come down to breakfast looking yellow about the eyes.

I fancy that life is more amusing now than it was forty years ago and I have a notion that people are more amiable. They may have been worthier then, possessed of more substantial knowledge; I do not know. I know they were more cantankerous; they ate too much, many of them drank too much, and they took too little exercise. Their livers were out of order and their digestions often impaired.

The account of the first paragraph, which is Butler, is pitched in a key identical with that of the second, which is Maugham. The effect in both is gained by a series of apparently matter-of-fact statements, made almost off-hand, with a sort of casual formality, qualified by a sort of airy, " Of course I don't really know. Don't go and take my word for it," which in reality injects the note of irony. Maugham and Butler again and again use this trick of creating ironic effect by disclaiming all trustworthy knowledge of what they are talking about, and by pitching their remarks in a negative key. The effect is delicious; butter won't melt in these acid mouths. *The Way of All Flesh* and *Cakes and Ale* will, in fact, repay some pretty close comparative study, and will show, I think, that Maugham found a far more profitable and compatible influence in Butler than in Maupassant.

It is my contention in fact that if Maugham had, as

a writer of stories, rejected Maupassant as a model and
kept more closely to Butler, we should have been presented with the first full-length English short-story
writer worthy of comparison with the best continental
figures. Unfortunately Maugham, in spite of an excellent eye, a dispassionate steadiness, a genius for the
diagnosis of human frailty, and a cosmopolitan temperament, lacks one very great and supremely important
quality. Unlike Tchehov and Maupassant, in whom he
professes to see great differences but who were much
alike at least in this respect, Maugham lacks compassion.
He has no heart, and in place of that heart one has the
impression that he uses a piece of clockwork. It is this,
I think, that gives Maugham's work the frequent impression of cheapness. This effect is heightened by
something else. Maugham, having mastered the art of
irony, mistakenly supposed himself to be a cynic. But
throughout Maugham's work, and notably in the stories,
there exists a pile of evidence to show that Maugham the
cynic is in reality a tin-foil wrapping for Maugham the
sentimentalist. Maugham's cynicism indeed peels off
under too-close examination, thin, extraneous, tinny,
revealing underneath a man who is afraid of trusting and
finally of revealing his true emotions.

There would be little point, here, in doing more than
summarize the quality of Maugham's stories. They are
easily available, pleasantly readable ; they tell a story—
in the sense, that is, that what they have to say can be
expressed anecdotally ; they deal largely with romantic
places, for Maugham, like Kipling and Conrad, loves the

East, and to his talent for painting its scenery and people he owes, as they do, much of his popular success. He delights in exposing human frailty, particularly amorous and marital frailty, and the humbug of convention ; he is suave and urbane ; he has the keenest sense of dramatic situations and delights in leaving the reader, as Maupassant and O. Henry did, with the point of the story neatly sharpened and vinegared in his hands. His natural sense of poetry is nil; his methods are as objective as the newspaper report of a court case, and sometimes as bad ; he wisely refrains, except on rare occasions, from the purple passage, yet he has apparently never discovered any conscious and simple method of detecting himself in the act of using a cliché. When he is good, like the little girl, he is very good ; and similarly when he is bad he is horrid.

Maugham indeed, though presenting the interesting case of a man who (on his own confession) evolved an attractively individual style without the help of a natural ear for words, has nothing new to offer. He simply perpetuates a tradition of straightforward, objective story-telling, largely derived from French naturalism, that is already well known. Thus Maugham's influence is not, and never has been, wide or important.

It is precisely for this reason that he is included, with Conrad, in a chapter designed primarily to show something of the first influences that were shaping the post-Great War short story. Neither Conrad nor Maugham, for all their popularity and excellence, contributed any lasting momentum to the short story's progress. The same may be said of their contemporaries. Galsworthy and Bennett, maintaining in their best work a sound tradition of realistic craftsmanship that should not (in Bennett especially) be underestimated, also wrote stories ; so did W. H. Hudson (the volume *El Ombú* is excellent) ; so did many other well-known and well-liked writers of the day. But none threatened the orderly business of that day, as Joyce did, with a charge of dynamite ; or the complacent patient, as Lawrence did, with a hypodermic injection of disturbing virulence. Conrad, Maugham, Bennett, Galsworthy, Hudson, and the many writers of their generation simply carried over into the new world the cooled and now unmalleable traditions of the old. For them it was too late to change ; it was too late to be revolutionary. They left the art of the novel in general on a higher shelf than they had first found it : little more. The most important influences on the short story were to come, as always, from abroad.

Chapter VII

THE IRISH SCHOOL

THE English language has a quality of porousness; it is constantly in a state of receptive plasticity. The easy absorption of influences from abroad, the readiness to incorporate new patterns of speech, are things which keep the language from getting cold. Yet it is a remarkable thing that it is outside England, notably on the American continent and in Ireland, that the English language, both spoken and written, now shows its most vigorous and most plastic vitality.

This has been true of Irish writing for many years. A natural genius for dramatizing life, for expressing the commonest emotion by means of a kind of poetic declamation, finds natural expression in Irish but very rarely in English letters. Take away the expression of the Irish genius from English literature, if only in the drama (Sheridan, Goldsmith, Shaw, Synge, Yeats, O'Casey), and the stock of that literature suffers a considerable fall. Do the same to the English short story of the past forty years (George Moore, Joyce, O'Flaherty, O'Connor, O'Faoláin, and others) and the result is much the same.

The Irish short story has been bred of vastly different qualities from the English. Where art and people fight for existence, whether against religious, moral, or political tyranny or against plain indifference, and where such art is naturally poetic and such people are naturally and proudly belligerent, the tendency of all expression is bound to be revolutionary. Nor is poetry, in Ireland, regarded as something like a certificate of insanity. I remember how, listening to a play by O'Casey, I commented that no back-street Dublin washerwoman would ever in her natural life talk with the extravagant moon-and-star metaphors that O'Casey put into her mouth ; and being instantly, bitterly, and rightly reproved by an Irishman for not knowing that such metaphor was the blood in the veins of all common Irish speech. Politics too have shaped Irish letters as they have not shaped English. For whereas internal politics, in Ireland, sooner or later mean some sort of internal bloodshed, the English, always regarded by the Irish as plain fools or knaves, know better. Like the Germans, the Japanese, and the Italians, the English know better than to fight their wars on their own soil, and for centuries have very conveniently settled their differences on the European mainland, in Asiatic passes, and on African deserts—where, as I have pointed out, the writers of the day were otherwise too occupied to intrude. In England, Scotland, and Wales political differences never reach a point where they need to be expressed in a drama more violent than words. Secret arms, bombs, subversive dynamite, revolutionary revolvers are weapons the English are always careful enough never to use on themselves. In Ireland they are the natural expression of political disagreement—a disagreement that for ever has some part of its causes in England. In consequence, as Miss Elizabeth Bowen has pointed out, " on the Irish side, indignation has been fruitful ; the long hopeless romantic quarrel has bred literature." [1]

One other influence, entirely absent as a mass influence on English literature, works like a common uneasy leaven throughout Irish letters—the Catholic church. In a brief but very illuminating study of James Joyce, Mr. L. A. G. Strong (part Irish himself) discusses what stands behind *Ulysses*—" behind it, in direct line, even more inescapably than the *Odyssey* which has given it its form, and the French writers who suggested its technique, the *Divina Commedia*, and the Inquisition," [2] and marks among other things, " the sense of sin, that terrific legacy which the Catholic Church irrevocably leaves her children." The consequent struggle between the artist and religion, between religion and experience, though more positive and agonized in Joyce than in any other writer, is a heritage that infuses a greater part of the best Irish writing with a quality of poetic mysticism ; and in all of the writers of stories discussed in this chapter, from Moore to O'Faoláin, there can be seen, in some degree, an expression of the struggle between beauty and sin, between the legacy of moral superstition and the physical loveliness of life, a struggle that gives them all the attitude of men sensuously grasping and caressing at the flesh of life while fearfully glancing over

[1] Elizabeth Bowen : intro. *The Faber Book of Modern Stories* (Faber)
[2] L. A. G. Strong : *English Novelists*, ed. Verschoyle (Chatto)

their shoulders for the dark swirl of the benighting cassock.

This is the continuous internal influence that frets the Irish writer. It is not surprising, perhaps, that the predominant external influence on Irish letters has therefore, for the past fifty years at least, been French. The modern Irish short story might be said to owe its existence, in fact, to the spell cast on the young and impressionable George Moore by the French naturalists, and to the subsequent publication of Moore's own stories in *The Untilled Field*. This book, appearing in 1903, shortly after the Boer War (England was then hateful, remarks Moore), had a success that should not discourage those who to-day believe the short story is unpopular. It sold a hundred copies. In a preface to a later edition Moore indulges in one of those precious nostalgic reminiscences so dear to his heart, and claims for the book that it was, as the major source of Synge's *The Playboy of the Western World*, "a landmark in Anglo-Irish literature, a new departure." Since there is no means of safely checking the importance of Moore as a revolutionary influence on Synge's literary life, we may leave Synge out of it and take Moore's claim for the book at its face value. And the claim is true.

Like many new departures, Moore's effort in *The Untilled Field* now looks exceedingly and deceptively simple. Viewed in relation to their period, however, these stories are, as Mr. L. A. G. Strong says of Joyce's own unwanted stories twenty years later, a portent. For *The Untilled Field*, unless I am very greatly mistaken, had some hand in the parentage of *Dubliners*, itself perhaps the most distinguished landmark in the history of the English short story. Moore himself speaks of having learned " the art of presentation " in Paris, and the word is significant. For what Moore did was to break away from the popular convention of telling a story by means of unravelling a series of artificial (moral, scientific, detective) dilemmas, and turn back to the presentation of common lives and to shaping his stories, as it were, out of natural common clay. The chance that nobody would take any notice is confirmed by the number of copies sold. Yet these stories of the Irish peasantry, the country priests, the exiles in America, have to-day a fresh exquisite realism that shows no sign, and I think will continue to show no sign, of the mildew that gathers so quickly even on the best of artificial products. Moreover, in an age still not free of the shackles of heavy prose tradition, these stories of Moore's are *short* stories : economical, pared down, light in structure, transparent. They have the natural poetry of earth and will remain, as Moore hoped they would remain, models for the future.

This is not quite so true of Moore's later stories, which tended to grow longer and more exquisitely elaborate as Moore's love of his own voice became more and more a precious obsession. The nostalgic and sensuous love of words, not only for their own sakes but for their evocative associations, is something which grew on Moore as it grew, far more powerfully, on Joyce, resulting in the complex incantations of his dream vocabularies. Moore sought to purify language, to refine the art of story-telling, and in doing so only succeeded in producing a style about which there lingers a flavour of the lamp. The brief, telling, natural poetry of *The Untilled Field* gave way to the lingering melodic cooings of *Celibate Lives*, interesting examples of the *conte* and of a style, exquisite, individual but slightly false, which has some of the dreamy monotony of a sustained pedal note. I would not for a moment underestimate the beauties of Moore's later stories, but it is significant that it is on their exquisite surfaces that the dust begins to gather, and that the dew is still fresh on the natural earth of *The Untilled Field*.

Joyce was born in 1882, and so might well have read *The Untilled Field* when, as a young man in Dublin, he chose to train his powers as a writer instead of his exceptional tenor voice. Since this book was begun Joyce has died, to be mourned with rather bewildered obituary garlands inscribed largely to the memory of the author of *Finnigan's Wake* and *Ulysses*. In most of these notices little mention, and sometimes no mention at all, was made of Joyce's only volume of stories, *Dubliners*, written in a manner which Joyce never chose to repeat, but on which his reputation could safely stand even if, by some chance, *Ulysses* and the later symbolic dictionaries should be lost to posterity.

Dubliners, hawked in true popular literary tradition from publisher to publisher, was indeed, as Mr. Strong remarks again in his essay, a portent and revolution :

They pricked the fabric [says Mr. Strong] of the contemporary short story. Once they became part of the literary consciousness, the art of the short story underwent a change. For all their quietness, their drab tones, they are as violently original as anything written in this century.

The words "violently original" stand out in this estimate—in what lay this violent originality ? *Dubliners*, containing fourteen quite short stories and one long one, appeared in 1914, though the stories had been written a good deal earlier. Reading these stories to-day, a quarter of a century later, one is struck above all by their naturalness—overlaid, sometimes, by a most delicate formality of manner. The pictures of Dublin have a kind of smoky and tender line of reality, a haunting and feminine touch of mystery : for Dublin is Joyce's heroine. Yet there is another quality, for which there was in 1914 a precedent in the Irish short story but none in the English—poetry. The sensuous music of Joyce's prose is a sound that could never be heard in the work of Wells and Kipling and O. Henry :

A few light taps upon the pane made him turn to the window. It had begun to snow again. He watched sleepily the flakes, silver and dark, falling obliquely against the lamplight. The time had come to set out on his journey westward. Yes, the newspapers were right : snow was general all over Ireland. It was falling on every part of the

154

dark central plain, on the treeless hills, falling softly upon the Bog of Allen and, farther westward, softly falling into the dark mutinous Shannon waves.

There is no word in this passage that a child of ten could not understand, no picture that it could not at once assimilate. Its prevailing tone is one of poetic naturalness. Without trick or metaphor, but simply by using words as a musical notation which in turn transmits, as music will, a pictorial and emotional effect, Joyce weaves the spell of great beauty that hangs over the final pages of *The Dead*. Throughout the story, without doubt the greatest that ever came out of Ireland, that same method is pursued. The story is one of a Christmas party in Dublin. Through the festivity, the singing, the decorations, the gay supper, the conversations, there goes a man whose most earnest preoccupation during the evening is himself and the speech he will make at the supper table. The success of the party and his own part in it fill him with self-centred happiness. As the party is breaking up someone sings a song, " The Lass of Aughrim," and the man who is pleasantly puffed with his own success sees the effect of that song on his wife—" that there was colour in her cheeks and that her eyes were shining." And as they go home together in the dark evening in which snow is beginning to fall it is brought home to him that she is mourning for a boy who once sang that song, was in love with her, and died. His sudden sorrow, the realization of his own selfishness and the poor part he himself has played in her life, are the things which give the story not only its point, but something like a soul. No story which preceded it in English was written with such tender yet rigidly objective beauty ; nothing had ever had such musical and yet pictorial quality, or such refinement of emotion and atmosphere.

Here then, it seems to me, lies the secret of Joyce's originality. It is an originality arising not from ideas, clever manipulation of plots, startling events, terrific dilemmas, scientific mysteries. It is an originality arising solely from Joyce's power to transmute ordinary life (a Christmas party, a suicide, a drunken clerk, life in a boarding house, a jealous mother), to render it naturalistically and yet compassionately, objectively and yet with rare beauty of emotional tone. Such art, as Mr. Strong has pointed out, pricked the fabric of the contemporary story ; and not surprisingly. The contemporary story was still the complacent slave of ideas, of so-called masculinity of action, of carefully engineered dilemmas and crises affecting, largely, the lives of unreal people. Joyce, on the other hand, found the crises and dilemmas of life sufficiently terrible without having to invent or manipulate them. Like Moore, he had learned the art not only of presentation, but of filtering life through an extremely fine mesh of sensibility, and the result was such exquisite stuff as *The Dead*, *Clay*, *A Little Cloud*, *Araby*, and the rest, which were unfortunately never to be repeated in the years of Joyce's preoccupation with a more complex form.

So the most natural method of telling a story appeared, in 1914, the most revolutionary—and of course the most unwanted. *Dubliners*, succeeding only after immense difficulty in getting published at all, must have fallen like a solitary leaf on a world crackling with the sound of arms and hatreds; and a public reading *The First Hundred Thousand* could have no ear for such delicate individuality. No second edition appeared for eight years, by which time Ireland was in the bitter entanglement of its own revolutionary war, from which were to emerge three new short-story writers of importance.

Of these the first was Liam O'Flaherty, an Aran Islander of demonstrative and revolutionary temperament, who came to London and began to write in the early 1920's. O'Flaherty, like many another writer just beginning, had cosmopolitan notions of writing, wanted to let off political crackers, and instantly chose to write of the life (*i.e.* London) he knew least. O'Flaherty, greatly fancying himself as a tough realist, forgot the poet in himself and set out to reproduce the more lurid shades of Maupassant. His work was seen by Edward Garnett, who promptly dispatched O'Flaherty to Ireland, advised him to look at his own people and, in his own words, " write a story about a cow." From that very sensible advice there came a spate of vivid sketches and stories about Irish peasants and fishermen which had the freshness of new paint. From the birth of a lamb, the death of a cow, the first flight of a blackbird, the peasant hatred of brothers, even from the progression of an Atlantic wave gathering and hurling itself against the Aran rocks, O'Flaherty extracted a wild, tender, and sometimes violently nervous beauty. Untamed words were hurled like stabs of paint on the page ; the world of sea and craggy fields and animal peasants was seen, like Maupassant's, in a vivid glare of light. Emotions here were primitive : passion, greed, physical violence, jealousy, hatred, love, hunger, poverty. Men and women moved with a raw animal fury and lust that was checked only by the inevitable fear of priestly wrath and the terrors of hell.

That world had much in common with Maupassant's, and O'Flaherty, as a novelist scrappy, sensational, and often cheap, had a keen and relentless eye for its colour, its drama, its contradictory forces of greed and religion, simplicity and craftiness, devotion and deception, and not least its primitively beautiful background of sea, earth, and sky. In consequence his stories give the effect of pictures dynamically conceived and flashed on a screen. The leisurely refined compassion of Joyce is missing ; the precious musical periods of Moore are absent. Everything has in it a kind of impatient sting, a direct stabbing physical force, brutal, sensuous, and elemental.

The achievement of *Spring Sowing*, *The Tent*, *The Mountain Tavern* was notable—and was not continued. O'Flaherty, famous for a period as the author of *The Informer* and other novels, slipped out of the English literary scene for a life of international wandering. The loss was most notably the short story's : for if Joyce's stories had been revolutionary in a quiet way,

O'Flaherty's were revolutionary in a way that could, like Maupassant's, have done much to popularize the short story. For O'Flaherty, like Maupassant, saw life in a strong light, dramatically, powerfully. Energy alone is not enough, but the sensuous poetic energy of O'Flaherty was like a flood ; the reader was carried away by it and with it, slightly stunned and exalted by the experience. *The Dead*, unless I am mistaken about the future of the reading public and its taste, will always be read by the few ; but O'Flaherty was the born popular writer.

O'Flaherty, after taking part in the Great War, became a man of Communist sympathies. Whether he took part in the Irish rebellion I do not know, but it is certain that his two most notable successors, Sean O'Faoláin and Frank O'Connor, were comrades in that struggle : secretly bearing arms, hiding in farmhouses, making bombs, avoiding the armoured patrols of the Tans, continually on the run across the sleepy beautiful Irish countryside. Such experience as theirs, disjointed, secret, dangerous, dramatic, the outcome of passionate hatreds and loyalties, cries out to be expressed in two forms— in drama, which O'Casey did so admirably, and in poetic narrative, which for another generation might have meant the ballad but which for O'Connor and O'Faoláin meant the short story. Both men belonged to that generation which felt its youth to be disrupted ; both were poets robbed of any pretty ambitions towards conventional lyricism by a world that, in O'Casey's words, was in a " terrible state o' chassis." Both found their medium in the short story, where the bitterness of the revolution could be dramatized against a background of haunting natural beauty.

This last sentence is truer of O'Faoláin's first and most important volume, *Midsummer Night Madness*, than of Frank O'Connor's *Guests of the Nation*. O'Faoláin is of Southern Ireland, and in him there is none of the wild-eyed Aran Islander who sees life in a strong elemental glare and whose God is Maupassant. O'Faoláin was attracted naturally, and rightly, to writers of dreamier, more delicate quality—on the one hand Turgenev, on the other George Moore. Like them, he had a rare gift of transferring the colour and scent of natural landscapes to paper, a rare susceptibility to feminine beauty : qualities which give his work a sensuous texture, extremely beautiful. Those qualities are seen to perfection in the story *Midsummer Night Madness*, where the young revolutionary watches the drama of a young and beautiful girl and an old man in a remote country house, in the remarkable *Small Lady*, and in *Fugue*, where one of two revolutionaries on the run sees an enchanting girl at a lonely farmhouse and longs to stay but knows he must go inexorably and hopelessly on. Behind these stories and all the others of that first notable volume, the drama of the revolution beats restlessly against the background of tender Irish mists and mountains and through the hushed streets of Cork. To the same drama Frank O'Connor brought less poetry, a more rational, more objective, more impatient personality : so that his stories are, so to speak, less steeped in the wine of Irish atmosphere. Yet they too are excellent—strongly Irish, made of the stuff of organic life, dramatic, humorous, beautiful.

These volumes are, then, the structure on which the Irish short story is built : *The Untilled Field, Dubliners, Spring Sowing, Midsummer Night Madness, Guests of the Nation.* Unparalleled in English—partly because in England there is no Dublin, no revolution, no Catholic Church—they are nevertheless part of the backbone of the English short story too. They are the new story : the story which is not a jig-saw puzzle of artificial properties that the reader is invited to piece together in order to make a whole and satisfactory picture of two dimensions, but the story in which the author stakes everything on his transposition of the life about him and his ability to make of that life a four-dimensional picture. If I have discussed the Irish development before the English in this respect, it is because it seems to me that the Irish temperament was quicker in its response to the new method—if indeed it was new at all—than the English. For Moore and Joyce precede the renaissance of Katherine Mansfield and Coppard by some years, as they precede the renaissance brought about by Sherwood Anderson in America. The singular thing is that the impetus given to the Irish short story by the Rebellion expended its momentum very quickly, whereas the impetus given by Sherwood Anderson (via Hemingway and others) to the new American story is still very powerfully in motion. That impetus was felt, and continues to be felt, in England, even though England gives little opportunity for the regional story, for impressing on it, so to speak, the local accent. The progress of the Irish movement is meanwhile arrested. New and refreshing momentum is seen instead from an unexpected quarter—Wales—and will be discussed later.

CHAPTER VIII

AMERICAN RENAISSANCE

To a young English writer beginning somewhere about 1921 the business of writing stories, the only possible source of modern American inspiration would have been the author of *Winesburg Ohio*. The story of Sherwood Anderson, who has recently died, is perhaps well known—how, after the war, in the years of immediate bewilderment, he began to write stories which broke free from all past American tradition and stereotyped formalism, how no important editor of the day was interested in these stories, and how they appeared, for the most part, in obscure magazines. To what has been called the frozen literary convention of the day the behaviour of Anderson must indeed have looked a little queer. The American short-story writer of that period had evolved an easily stencilled formula for his work, and was busy making money by running off the well-made two-dimensional sheets. His models were writers of his own class in England, the appeal was cosmopolitan, the convention hollow. "He evolved situations out of abstractions and clothed lay figures to act as the puppets in his marionette theatre." [1]   How long this sterile con-

[1] E. J. O'Brien : intro. *Best Short Stories, 1933* (Cape)

vention would have gone on untouched if it had not been for Anderson it is impossible to say.

Anderson realized two things : first that the United States was not a country but a continent and that, in his own words, " in it are to be found so many different conditions of life, so many different social traditions that the writer who attempts to express in his work something national is in an almost impossible situation." And second, that if ever there were to be an American literature, in an American tradition, the first act of the American writer must be to turn his back on Europe, break with its conventions and begin the task of exploring and presenting the lives of his own people. Now, of course, when two decades of writers have done much to put Anderson's theory into practice, it all sounds extremely simple. Yet during the course of a hundred and fifty years of American literature hardly a writer had conceived the same simple notion—the notion, among other things, that " California is not Maine. North Dakota is not Louisiana. Ohio is not North Carolina," and that " we are as yet strangers to each other." Anderson knew that a writer could remain in one place, paint its apparently colourless and unimportant life and yet depict, as Jane Austen did, a whole world.

I have used the word " paint " deliberately, for this was something else that Anderson realized—that (and again it was very simple) the writer can say all he wants to say in pictures. The result was that " almost for the first time, an American artist . . . attempted in his fiction to present a picture rather than to write an

ephemeral play," though " the pictorial values of Sherwood Anderson's work were not at first apparent, because his pictures lacked colour. He was much more
concerned to present significant form than to dazzle the
eye with colour." [1] Anderson indeed, for all his slow,
subdued, colourless tone was a man in revolt, and part
of the effect of that revolt was to bring the writer into a
closer, more sensuous contact with his material and in
particular to enable the American writer to break with
what Anderson himself called the " cold, hard and
stony culture " of New England, " in which gentility
and respectability became the passion of our writers."
Anderson in fact was resolved to set down the life of the
American middle-west not as the aristocratic New England culture had wanted to see it, as a " preparation for
a life after death," not as something in which every act
had inescapable moral causes and consequences, but as
a moving organic pattern, however stupid, colourless,
designless, cruel, depraved, and ultimately frustrated it
might seem to be.

That method, so simple and yet so revolutionary when
seen in relation to the period, was applied by Anderson
to people that had never before had conferred on them
the dignity of literature : the poor whites of the Ohio
valleys, remote farmers, the negroes and boys that hang
around race tracks, obscure dreamers in the back streets
of Chicago, country school-teachers and lawyers of
frustrated ambition living in the desolate dust of forgotten townships. Of their lives Anderson had nothing

[1] E. J. O'Brien : intro. *Best Short Stories, 1938* (Cape)

to say that was romantic. He saw them thoughtfully, with bemused detachment, with a certain melancholy heaviness behind which glowed a constant kindliness of heart. Undetained and unguided by him, these people moved past the office-windows of the young reporter watching in *Winesburg Ohio*, up and down the hard Chicago streets, through lives that led " out of nowhere into nothing." Anderson set down what he saw and felt about them with a kind of tender bewilderment, as if he were really as troubled by their negation and stupidity and colourless frustration as they were, in a style handled with apparent casualness, off-hand, so that its charm arose from what seemed to be a studied stylelessness.

Both the rewards and the dangers of this method are obvious. By a public instructed largely in a literature where characters were stereotyped as good or bad, and the physical processes of life, and especially love, were rendered by means of a patent formula, Anderson was of course branded as immoral. This was natural, and is now irrelevant. The real danger of Anderson's method was that it lay wide open to parody, which Anderson himself accomplished to some extent in *Dark Laughter*, unintentionally, of course, and which Hemingway completed in *Torrents of Spring*. This too, I think, does not matter. In Anderson there is a weakness arising from a certain lack of self-censorship. He lacks the austerity that would prevent him from revelling in the luxury of an emotion. But it does not and cannot detract from the inspirational force of Anderson's example to the short story of his day. *Winesburg Ohio* is the first directional signpost of the contemporary American short story, directing the writer to turn inward to the job of establishing, out of indigenous American material, a new American tradition.

The ultimate effect of Anderson's pioneering example was a release of energy that was to have, during the next fifteen or twenty years, immense creative results. The immediate effect was its influence on Ernest Hemingway : for if Anderson stopped creating stories by the old facile methods of stereotyping, Hemingway broke up every known type-face with which the American short story had ever been set, and cut for it a more austere, revolutionary, and yet more classic design than it had ever known. In doing so Hemingway brought down a hammer on all writing done to a fancy design ; he stripped of its impossible periodic splendour that style of writing which reaches its limits in the intricacies of Henry James ; he sheared away the literary woolliness of English as no one had ever done before.

Like Anderson, Hemingway began publishing obscurely, during the private-press vogue of the early twenties, and some of his stories appeared privately in Paris, where it is obvious that he came under the influence of Gertrude Stein. Somewhere between Stein and Anderson, however, there was a middle course, and Hemingway took it. Hemingway had sense enough to see that it might be a million years before there was a public initiated enough to read its fiction in the bony theoretical rhythms offered by Miss Stein. You cannot feed a public on fancy literary theorems, and Hemingway, who had plenty to say, wanted a public. He took the Stein method, which at its most aggravated seemed to have some appeal to mental deficiency, and, as it were, put sanity into it. For every person who· read Stein, pretending to understand it whether he did or not, a potential million could read Hemingway.

His first story, *Up in Michigan*, was written in Paris in 1921, and as far as I know there is no record that it caused a sensation. It was collected, together with another fifteen stories, into the volume *In Our Time*, and again I know of no record that a revolution was caused. Yet a revolution had been caused, and in these stories, less good and less famous than the contents of *Men Without Women* though they are, the Hemingway method is already in conscious and advanced production.

What is that method ? Why did it cause a revolution ? In the first place Hemingway was a man with an axe. For generations—it might almost be said for a hundred years or more—written English had been growing steadily more pompous, more prolix, more impossibly parochial ; its continuous tendency had been towards discussing and explaining something rather than projecting and painting an object. It carried a vast burden of words which were not doing a job, and it was time, at last, to cut those words away. In the 'nineties Samuel Butler too had arrived with an axe, but it was an axe less against English writing than against English morality, and Butler had never dramatized the conflict except in a single book. Hemingway, looking back over what still purports to be the great age of the English novel, must have been struck by an interesting fact, of which there are most notable examples in Hardy. He must have been struck by the fact that out of the cavernous gloom of explanations, discussions, social dilemmas, and philosophizings all that emerged of permanent interest and value were the scattered bright scraps of pictorial narrative. In one generation the philosophy had grown mouldy, the social dilemmas were forgotten for others, the moral currency had been changed. But the people, the narrative action, the colour of scenes, remained, and could, if properly conceived and painted, never fade. So what one remembers out of Hardy, for example, is not the philosophic vapourings or the spiritual anguish, all impossibly unreal to-day, but the sharp bright scenes that have been painted by a man with his eye on the object— the pig-sticking in *Jude*, Tess working in the winter turnip field, Tess praying with the children, the man selling his wife in *The Mayor of Casterbridge*. No changing currency of social and moral action changes these ; nothing can come between them and countless generations of readers.

What Hemingway went for was that direct pictorial contact between eye and object, between object and reader. To get it he cut out a whole forest of verbosity. He got back to clean fundamental growth. He trimmed off explanation, discussion, even comment ; he hacked off all metaphorical floweriness ; he pruned off the dead, sacred clichés ; until finally, through the sparse trained words, there was a view.

The road of the pass was hard and smooth and not yet dusty in the early morning. Below were the hills with oak and chestnut trees, and far away below was the sea. On the other side were snowy mountains.

The picture is complete. And again :

The hills across the valley of the Ebro were long and white. On this side there was no shade and no trees and the station was between two lines of rails in the sun. Close against the side of the station there was the warm shadow of the building and a curtain, made of strings of bamboo beads, hung across the open door into the bar, to keep out flies.

And here is a portrait, with background, complete :

An old man with steel-rimmed spectacles and very rusty clothes sat by the side of the road. There was a pontoon bridge across the river and carts, trucks, and men, women and children were crossing it. The mule-drawn carts staggered up the steep bank from the bridge with soldiers helping push against the spokes of the wheels. The trucks ground up and away heading out of it all and the peasant plodded along in the ankle deep dust. But the old man sat there without moving. He was too tired to go any farther.

The pictures projected are as natural as life. There are no attempts at falsification, no superimposed colours, no rose glasses, no metaphors. Everything that could cloud or date the scene has been ruthlessly rejected. Examine by contrast :

No sooner did the rays of the rising sun shine on the dew, and fall in little fiery tongues upon their eyelids, than instinct made them strike camp and move away. All day they would journey, until the setting sun made the air to glow like a damp fire, burning the eyes while it chilled the body. The moon, like a disc of copper, hung behind them and the plain seemed dead. [1]

Here the effort to influence the reader is strenuous. Hemingway in effect says " here is the picture. That's all. Keep your eye on it " ; and is prepared to trust the reader to absorb the proper impression. But Mr. Sitwell cannot trust the reader. The light must be changed, trick-focused, dimmed or raised for a series of effects. Each sentence has its metaphor ; each metaphor is supported by some poetic archaism—" upon," " made the air to glow," " than instinct made them." The result is a decorative backcloth, looking real enough until the wind stirs it, and then suddenly ludicrous—what a Hemingway character would rightly call phoney.

But Hemingway carried this purge of style beyond mere description. For a century the novel had staggered along under the weight of a colossal convention of fancy mechanics in the matter of dialogue. The novel had managed somehow to survive it ; the short story had

[1] Sacheverell Sitwell : *The Gothick North* (Duckworth)

been in constant danger of collapsing. In this convention the words of a character had their intonation, flavour, emotion, or meaning underlined by the writer. Thus : " he reiterated with a manifest show of anger " ; " she ventured to remark with a melancholy intonation in her voice " ; " he declared haltingly " ; " he stammered out in frightened accents " ; " he interposed " ; " he interjected with a low laugh," and so on and so on. Wads of this verbal padding bolstered up the conversation of every novel from Dickens down to the fourpenny paperback.

Hemingway swept every letter of that convention away. In its place he put nothing but his own ability to imply, by the choice, association, and order of the words, whether a character was feeling and speaking with anger, regret, desperation, tenderness ; quickly or slowly ; ironically or bitterly. All intonation and emotion lay somewhere in the apparently abrupt and casual arrangement of the words ("I feel fine," she said. "There's nothing wrong with me. I feel fine."), and Hemingway asked nothing except the co-operation of the reader in the job of capturing these intonations and emotions.

A classic example of this method will be seen in the famous story *Hills Like White Elephants*. In that story a man is taking a girl to Madrid for an illegal operation. That fact is nowhere stated throughout the whole story, nor is the girl's terror and bitterness, nor in fact is any other emotion. The couple wait on the way-side station for the Madrid express ; it is very hot, they drink beer, and they talk. For the girl something has crumpled up,

and it is not only the past but the future. She is terri-
fied, and the story is one of the most terrible Hemingway or anyone else ever wrote. Yet throughout the
whole of it—a story largely projected through dialogue
—Hemingway makes no single attempt to influence the
readers' thoughts, impressions, or conclusions. He himself is never there; not for a single instant does he come
between object and reader.

This story, and others like *The Killers*, *The Undefeated*,
and *Fifty Grand*, finally fixed the legend of the Hemingway method. The legend was that Hemingway was
tough and unliterary, a dumb ox. The truth was the
opposite. Hemingway is as conscious a literary writer
as ever there was. Behind him, unless I am greatly
mistaken, stand the influences of Turgenev, Maupassant,
Sherwood Anderson, Stephen Crane, Defoe, and the
English of the Authorized Version.[1] The legend of
toughness arose from a failure to distinguish between
Hemingway and his characters : the inarticulate boxers,
the bull-fighters, the gangsters, the soldiers. They were
depicted as leading a life governed more or less without
thought ; they moved to ox-like instincts ; the world
is full of such people, and it is no use, as Hemingway
knew, putting fancy literary thoughts into their heads.
So Hemingway wrote about them in their own ox-like,
instinctive, thoughtless language, well knowing that his
greatest danger was sentimentalism, a danger he struggled

[1] It is interesting to compare Hemingway's method with that of
the New Testament in Basic English, recently issued ; in particular
with certain narrative passages in the Acts of the Apostles.

so hard to avoid that finally he fell over backwards, as it were, into an inverted form of it. For Hemingway is a deeply emotional writer. Underneath the crust of style, apparently so hard and arid, the deepest rhythms move like warm volcanic lava. He is above all a tragic writer, haunted, repelled, and attracted by the everlasting fear of mortality.

Perhaps no Protestant can pretend to understand the Catholic mind, and it is from Catholicism, perhaps, that Hemingway's constant preoccupation with the theme of death arises. His stories appear to deal with a variety of themes: boxing, bull-fighting, illegal operations, game-hunting, war, fishing; all of them physical subjects. But in reality Hemingway has only one theme—death. It is behind all but a fraction of his short stories; it is the whole subject of *Death in the Afternoon*; it is the climax towards which *A Farewell to Arms* inexorably moves. For Hemingway the twin ideas of physical activity and physical mortality are forces of a magnetism that never ceases its powerful attraction. As he remarks in *Death in the Afternoon*, " all stories, if continued far enough, end in death, and he is no true story-teller who would keep that from you." So death is the recurrent theme; the fear of it terrorizes Hemingway as the thought of being sentimental terrorizes him, until at last he is forced into it : death by gangsterism in *The Killers*, the man dying of gangrene in *The Snows of Kilimanjaro*, the fear of death in *Hills Like White Elephants*, death for the bull-fighter in *The Undefeated*, death for the Spanish boy in *The Capital of the World*.

174

For a time, in some of the shorter sketches, he escapes it, but sooner or later the magnetism of the eternal paradox that the flesh lives, and yet rots, draws him back again. The melancholy of it beats with rhythmic dying fall under the shell of the prose that has earned for itself, mistakenly, the reputation of being so imperviously tough :

> The boys picked up the cot and carried it around the green tents and down along the rock and out on to the plain and along past the smudges that were burning brightly now, the grass all consumed, and the wind fanning the fire, to the little plane.

Behind or beneath such a passage lies a personal rhythm that can never be imitated ; the rhythm of the man, the personal inward melancholy, the deep-rooted fear of death. It was this that the thousand imitators of Hemingway on both sides of the Atlantic could never recapture : for the little Hemingways, attracted by the easy street-corner toughness of the style, sprang up everywhere, slick copyists of the surface line, not one in a thousand of them understanding that the colder and harder a man writes, as Tchehov once pointed out, the more deeply and more movingly emotional is the result likely to be. Hemingway was in reality so deeply susceptible to emotion that he strove constantly for the elimination of himself, his thoughts and feelings, from the surface of the work. For that he was taken to task by Mr. Aldous Huxley, who represented the very intellectual aridity in writing that Hemingway was out to break ; Huxley accused Hemingway of belonging to a class of " intelligent and cultured people doing their best to feign stupidity and to conceal the fact that they have received an education."

Hemingway had a reply for that, and it was a good reply :

When writing a novel a writer should create living people ; people not characters. . . . If the people the writer is making talk of old masters ; of music ; of modern painting ; of letters, or of science then they should talk of these subjects in the novel. If they do not talk of these subjects and the writer makes them talk of them he is a faker, and if he talks about them himself to show how much he knows then he is showing off. No matter how good a phrase or a simile he may have if he puts it in where it is not absolutely necessary and irreplaceable he is spoiling his work for egotism. [1]

That statement is in reality as much a crack at Huxley and the arch-intellectuals who had become so over-educated that there was little in life that did not bore them with familiarity, as it is a defence of Hemingway himself and what he felt writing ought to be. Hemingway might have added that Huxley had never created a character, let alone a person, that was much more than a biological specimen being laid on the table for analytical

[1] *Death in the Afternoon*, p. 182 (Cape)

dissection. He might have added that though he himself dealt largely with people who were soon to be dead, the characters of Huxley were dead before Huxley ever dealt with them. What he did add was this :

> People in a novel, not skilfully constructed *characters*, must be projected from the writer's assimilated experience, from his knowledge, from his head, from his heart and from all there is of him.[1]

No statement of a writer's objects and intentions could be clearer ; and here it seems to me is the final proof, if proof is needed, that the legend of Hemingway's toughness (*i.e.* emotionlessness, dumbness, thick-skinnedness, etc.) had never any basis in fact. What Hemingway realized, and what it is important all short-story writers should realize, was that it is possible to convey a great many things on paper without stating them at all. To master the art of implication, of making one sentence say two or more different things, by conveying emotion and atmosphere without drawing up a tidy balance sheet of descriptions about them, is more than half the short-story writer's business. Because he mastered that business with a new staccato slickness of style, eliminating so much of what had been considered essential literary paraphernalia, Hemingway was and still is a most important writer.

Like all iconoclasts who break in on the stuffiness of their particular age with rude disregard for accepted behaviour, Hemingway was dangerous to imitate. It would be hard to assess the number of versions of *Hills Like White Elephants* received by editors during the last ten or fifteen years, but it would probably exceed the number of imitations of *Winesburg Ohio*. One-story writers in the Hemingway-Anderson manner popped up all over America just as one-book writers in the D. H. Lawrence manner popped up all over England. Both types in turn were never heard of again, but the fertilizing influence of Hemingway and Anderson went on.

The extent of that influence has been enormous. Anderson indicated that the American short-story writer had better practise self-denial in the matter of territory —he must be content with the regional, not the national, view ; Hemingway indicated that the American short-story writer should practise another kind of self-denial— the denial of irrelevant material, literary tricks, luxury emotions, literary descriptions, and literary faking. " If the writer of prose knows enough about what he is writing about he may omit things that he knows and the reader, if the writer is writing truly enough, will have a feeling of those things as strongly as though the writer had stated them." [1]

Inspired by such teaching, which incidentally achieved for the short story a new kind of commercial success, a whole generation of American short-story writers turned round to American earth, American cities, small

[1] *Ibid.*, p. 183

American towns, American homes, American politics, and American hopes and troubles, to find waiting for it the limitless untouched raw materials of a new American tradition. Writers had once shipped themselves, or had been shipped by anxious editors, to Cuba and Tahiti and Honolulu and other romantic spots in order to find something known as local colour. Now suddenly they found their local colour in Ohio valleys, in the fishing villages of Cape Cod, in San Francisco saloons, in Southern feuds between negro and white, in the Middle-West, on way-side hot-dog stands, on East Side New York, in Texas, indeed everywhere on their own multi-tongued conglomerous continent.

In writing of all this, they did something else which was significant. They took the language, which was still English, as they found it. They took it straight off the earth, the saloon-floor, the café table, the factory bench, the street, and the drug-store counter, not troubling to wipe off the colloquial dirt or the spittle, the common dust or the colour, the wit or the fantastically apt metaphor, the slickness or the slang. They took free speech and made it into free writing : a more flexible, more vital, more fluent writing, a braver and newer writing than ever the over-intellectualized writing of Mr. Huxley's *Brave New World* had known how to be.

And so, forced away from accepted literary tradition, pushed out of the study arm-chair, as it were, into the street, the American short story began at last to assume a more living shape, a shape cut out of raw tissue, of flesh and blood. And the number of writers who found in it their natural form of expression became, from 1925 onwards, very great. To deal with more than a fraction of them here would be a scrappy, unsatisfactory task. They came from all sections of America. From the South alone there emerged a whole literature, in which the clash of coloured and white, of decaying romanticism and the march of time, were predominant themes. The writer whose family roots, a generation back, had fed on the dirt of Central European ghettos or the soil of Central European fields was now an American citizen with something to say that had never been said by his inarticulate ancestors. As in England, a host of women writers emerged from the swift emancipation brought about by the Great War, and in increasing numbers they found the short story attractive. If I choose from these less than half a dozen representative names, it is not because I feel the rest are to be ignored. On the contrary, the whole field of the contemporary American story teems with nervous and energetic life ; it is being tilled by the tireless curiosity of scores of new writers who have discovered, thanks to Hemingway and Anderson, the amazing fertility of their native soil.

Among those writers I should say that William Faulkner, Erskine Caldwell, Katherine Ann Porter, and William Saroyan stand out. This is a considerable injustice to many other first-rate writers, all of whom handle the craft of the short story with a distinction it never came within miles of knowing a quarter of a century ago ; notably : Ruth Suckow, Kay Boyle,

Dorothy Parker, Willa Cather, Morley Callaghan, Manuel Komroff, John Steinbeck, William Marsh, Dorothy Canfield, and of course the humorists Leacock and Thurber.

Faulkner is contemporary with Hemingway. Of the same embittered generation, soured less by the futility of war than the aftermath, he is a disorientated romantic. His early stories dealt, like *A Farewell to Arms*, with the war in Europe, and were largely of flying ; in these stories he was striving, like Hemingway, to use a stricter, more rigidly muscular language than literature had previously known, but for various reasons he never mastered it. Language, and the emotion behind it, always mastered him ; Hemingway pruned the branches of his style until they stood clean as skeletons ; Faulkner began by pruning, only to allow the tree to break and blossom more prodigiously, so that at last he could luxuriate in its shade. As he went on, turning from the stories of war in Europe to stories of the older, perhaps still more cynical war in the Southern states, where white is at war with negro even down to the segregative notices in public places, Faulkner permitted himself more and more the luxury of a warmer, more emotional style. This gives his stories a certain shapelessness, almost florid beside the spare boniness of Hemingway, together with a quality of atmospheric passion and grandeur which Hemingway never aimed to achieve. Faulkner's subjects being what they are—the decaying Southern aristocracy, passionate spinsterhood, mass fury, racial injustice, murder, sexual conflict, and so on, and his backgrounds being what they are—the decaying Southern towns steeped by sunlight with a kind of ominous lethargy, this floridity, passion, and high atmospheric pressure all seem legitimate and in keeping. For Faulkner is primarily an atmospheric writer. His stories owe their life not to rigidity of structure, to clean energy of direction, to the denial of emotion, but to strength of mood. Once that mood is caught and then held by the corresponding rhythms of Faulkner's recklessly beautiful style, nothing can break it ; the emotional force must play itself out. The characters too are caught up by the dark forces of these moods, and are borne relentlessly on to tragic and predestined conclusions.

He went on, passing still between the homes of the white people, from street lamp to street lamp, the heavy shadows of oak and maple leaves sliding like scraps of black velvet across his white shirt. Nothing can look quite so lonely as a big man going along an empty street. Yet though he was not large, not tall, he continued somehow to look more lonely than a lone telephone pole in the middle of a desert. In the wide, empty, shadow-hooded street he looked like a phantom, a spirit, strayed out of its own world, and lost.[1]

The manner has a parallel in Conrad, whose characters also are shaped less by conscious and rational forces than by the vaguer, larger forces of atmosphere and destiny. And the characters too have a certain resemblance ; for

[1] *Light in August* (Chatto and Windus)

if Conrad reserves his deepest pity for the isolated, for men in lonely conflict against the forces of existence and destiny, Faulkner reserves his for the oppressed : the poor, the negroes, the beaten children, the frustrated, the decaying aristocracy, the frightened, and the framed. There is anger in his work : the social anger of a romantic gifted, or cursed, with a realistic pair of eyes. For Faulkner, like others of us, can never reconcile the opposing forces of existence, the justice and injustice, the simplicity and the cynicism, the beauty and the ugliness ; he can never align life as it is with life as it seems to be. Out of this natural and discomforting conflict arises the righteous moody anger of his work.

Such a manner, shaped by so much that is emotional, is bound to have many faults difficult to eradicate. In spite of these—a certain affected poeticism and turgidity. a striving for atmospheric effect, a tendency to introduce violence for its own sake, and some attempt at verbal experiment—Faulkner's stories must and should be read. He makes many mistakes, but they are the mistakes essential to a talent that cannot stand still. And it is interesting, I think, to read them against the stories of two other Southern writers, Erskine Caldwell and Katherine Ann Porter, whose backgrounds belong to the same world of poor whites, oppressed negroes, and dying aristocracy. After the turbulence of Faulkner, the work of Caldwell seems to have the transparent naïveté of an essay for a child's copy-book. Caldwell, like Hemingway, chose a race of characters that were not themselves articulate ; they did not talk, like Aldous Huxley's

characters, of philosophy and science, El Greco and
Matisse, communism and contraception. They were
simple types ; very simple, terribly simple ; close to
the animals and the earth from which they wrested a
miserable existence. Caldwell's problem in presenting
them was parallel with Hemingway's, and like him he
chose to present simplicity by simplicity, the inarticulate
by inarticulacy, dumbness by dumbness. He stripped
style of all its literary permutations and combinations
and made it work to the lowest common denominator :
simple, low-browed, casual almost to a point of
monotony, completely unpretentious and yet effective.
Its great danger was the danger that attended Hemingway
—that simplicity itself, if carried far enough, is only an
inverted form of affectation, just as toughness, if carried
far enough, is only an inverted form of sentimentalism.
But it is possible to allow Caldwell to escape the charge,
as Hemingway escapes it, because there is no denying
the quality of the mind behind the style. Those who may
incline to distrust Caldwell's pictures of the South, to
charge him with over-simplifying and over-brutalizing
that life, should glance at a book in which there have
been recorded, by photograph, the faces of some of the
people, negro and white alike, of whom the Caldwell
stories are only a partial record. That awful indictment
of American civilization, *You Have Seen Their Faces*, has
in it the quality that lies behind the all-too-deceptive
inarticulate flatness of *God's Little Acre*, *We Are the
Living*, and *American Earth* : an evangelical pity and
fervour.

Miss Katherine Ann Porter is a contrast to both Faulkner and Caldwell, though the background of her work, like theirs, is largely the South. In a sense she is the most accomplished writer, yet not the most individual writer, of the short story in America to-day. Her accomplishment is that of an amazing versatility. The charge that can be most often brought against the American short-story writer is that of limited perfection ; he often arrives, like Crane or Saroyan, fully equipped, all technical lessons learnt, only to be incapable of ever developing another inch. In the struggle to be heard at all, the American short-story writer knows that the un-trained voice is useless ; he trains hard, becomes capable of smooth achievement within a certain range of notes and, like Saroyan, contrives to repeat the same songs under new and catchy titles. One patent fault of the regional story is that it imposes limitations and may keep a writer incourageous, preventing him from committing the faults of experiment and adventure. A writer may feel bound to continue to reflect the life of a limited, perfectly known territory, knowing the results will be truthful and safe ; whereas climbing the fence will involve him in problems and perhaps disaster. Crane never climbed that fence ; nor, after eight books, has Saroyan showed the slightest sign of doing so.

For Miss Porter there are no fences, either territorial or social, technical or psychological. In a single volume of hers, *Pale Horse, Pale Rider*, she discloses a complete mastery over three sections of American territory ; and these are only a slight indication of her range. The reader of *Old Mortality*, a lavender family portrait of Southern aristocracy, or of *The Old Order*, a companion piece (" they talked about religion, and the slack way the world was going nowadays, the decay of behaviour, and about the younger children, whom these topics always brought at once to mind "), would set Miss Porter down as a painter of romantic domestic interiors done with deep firm charm and fragrant period accuracy, but little more. Here would seem to be a prime example of limited perfection painting over and over again the same subject with delicate affection and care. In a single story Miss Porter shatters the illusion. *Noon Wine* turns out to be a picture done on sackcloth ; lavender is replaced by muck ; the charming ruminations of old ladies by the spit of tobacco ; the tender rhythmical style by, " Well, him and me fell out over a plug of tobacco. He might just shove him anyhow and then tell people he was a fat man not used to the heat and while he was talking he got dizzy and fell off by himself, or something like that, and it wouldn't be the truth either, because it wasn't the heat and it wasn't the tobacco." This story of a murder on a Southern farm is as masculine as Hemingway ; it beats Mr. Steinbeck on his own territory ; its art is just as physical as theirs, and yet is fuller, more conscious and less naïve. Tchehov once said that he could write a story about anything, and for the Miss Porter who records the angry and harmless ruminations of old ladies with the same smooth skill as she throws off this drama of peasant violence there are equally no terrors of subject. As if to emphasize that versatility she produces in *Pale Horse, Pale Rider* itself a recreation of the atmospheric tension of the America of 1918; a cynical story of the war, of a girl falling in love with a soldier who dies from the disease he contracts from her. To each of these stories Miss Porter brings a style that is warmly malleable, that can be shaped and used as the subject demands : smooth and cultured and feminine, masculine and tough, sophisticated and cynical. She never imposes a single private style, as it were, on a whole succession of unrelated subjects. In the work of many women writers, notably Katherine Mansfield, Virginia Woolf, and Elizabeth Bowen, the private voice is never still ; it flutters and colours the surface of the style, imposing its influence. The voice of Miss Porter never obtrudes, yet is always there, flexible and objective, casting, directing, shaping the progress of the tale.

A writer of Miss Porter's diverse sympathies and technical flexibility may one day, perhaps, speak for all America; and there seems to be no reason why that writer should not be herself. Unlike William Saroyan, she cuts no capers on the way to success. Saroyan irresistibly recalls the market-place. He is the Eastern carpet-seller in a foreign country armed with the gift of the gab, a packet of psychological conjuring tricks, and a bunch of phoney cotton carpets from which, unexpectedly, he now and then produces a genuine Ispahan. He is too good a salesman not to be interested in everything that interests the customer : love, horses, women, little children, hunger, heartache, beauty, hope, money, poverty, God, and all the rest of the big bad crazy world, and these subjects, plus Mr. Saroyan, are the patter from which his stories are made.

Saroyan arrived in the early thirties with *The Daring Young Man on the Flying Trapeze*. A young American-Armenian, living in San Francisco, Saroyan proceeded to unfold a range of very dazzling carpets of tricky design, and while displaying them, talked the heads off the American public. Saroyan even then had nothing to learn technically. He arrived with every gag worked out, smooth, efficient, attractive, humorous, full of the cheek that gets on. Every story was a carpet that had to be sold, and talk would sell it :

> I hadn't had a haircut in forty days and forty nights, and I was beginning to look like several violinists out of work. You know the look : genius gone to pot, and ready to join the Communist Party. We barbarians from Asia Minor are hairy people : when we need a haircut, we *need* a haircut. It was so bad, I had outgrown my hat. (I am writing a serious story, perhaps one of the most serious I shall ever write. That is why I am being flippant. Readers of Sherwood Anderson will begin to understand what I am saying after a while ; they will know that my laughter is rather sad.) I was a young man in need of a haircut, so I went down to Third Street (San Francisco), to the Barber College, for a fifteen cent haircut.

Most of Saroyan is in that paragraph : the slick, arresting, straight beginning, the wise-crack (putting the audience in good humour), the touch of personal history and racial loyalty (" we Armenians," etc.), the diversion (generally literature, art, politics), and the final touch of narrative realism, just sufficient to move the scene from one point to another. There is no nonsense here about self-effacement, pure objectivity, etc. Saroyan is up in the front, talking; he is about to try to bamboozle you (and will succeed) into listening to a series of reflections, some serious, some saucy, some ironical, mostly deliberately irresponsible, on the state of the world as it seems to a man having a fifteen-cent haircut in San Francisco in the year of the depression, nineteen-thirty-five. It might just as well be Chicago, a ten-cent plate of soup, and the year nineteen-thirty-six. Scenes, places, and time itself do not matter very much, since nothing much is going to happen except that at the end of the story Saroyan will still be talking. There are no characters as such. People pop in and out of the scene as they pop in and out of a shop; they are met on the side-walk, in the barber's chair; they talk and Saroyan discusses what they have to say. Saroyan talks very fast, with colour, with many diversions, and with slick and entertaining knowledge of many subjects. Finally, as you turn to say something yourself, to seek elucidation perhaps on the value of the goods, it is suddenly to discover that Saroyan has folded up and discreetly departed, leaving you after a very engaging entertainment with something you never intended to buy.

What you have bought, if you intended to buy a story, appears to have little value. As a narrative,

measured by conservative standards, by the rule of
Kipling, Bret Harte, or even Hemingway, it is ludicrous.
As a sequence of trivialities of which the deeper significance is subtly implied, it leaves Tchehov himself
looking very old-fashioned. There is no plot, no heart-
stirring action, no dénouement. The world is crazy
enough, Saroyan thinks, without these things : there's
a ready-made plot in any barber's chair, and it never can
and never will be unravelled ; let's investigate *that* and
see what it looks like. It's a strange, crazy, disorderly
affair, true, when you put it down on paper—but why
should literature attempt to rob life of its disorderliness ?
By putting down the craziest, most chaotic bits of life we
may discover some truth—on the same principle that it
often comes out of the mouths of drunken men. Generations of writers have been tying life into neat bundles and
putting these bundles on to shelves where they now lie
forgotten under dust. I, says Saroyan, object to tying
up life into bundles ; on the contrary I want to release
it, to ferret it out, to knock the conventional, literary
stupid dust off it and set it free. Let's have done with
pretentiousness, neatness, good manners, order, serious-
ness and so-called sanity. Nothing in this world of contradictory values, of sublimity and rottenness, beauty
and cynicism, kindness and hatred, adds up to any sense
anyway, and who knows but what, after all, the lunatic
may not be the sanest man alive ? Who knows but what
lunacy may not be the clearest, calmest, most beautiful
kind of sanity ?

All this is very salutary and very refreshing ; every

generation needs a writer who puts his tongue out, and among other things Saroyan has shown yet one more phase of the short story's limitless possibilities. But Saroyan's method creates its own dangers. The first of these is monotony, Saroyan's stories being very short and capable of swift, easy, and frequent repetition; the second is exactly that which confronted Hemingway, and which Hemingway himself has become increasingly aware of and has, in later stories, done something to avoid—the danger that unpretentiousness, if deliberate enough and studied enough, may itself become a pose. Saroyan's revolt is the revolt of the young man who, hating the bowler hats, butterfly collars, and pin-stripe trousers of convention, himself puts on the green shirt, scarlet tie, and amber trousers of a new and brighter simplicity. Saroyan cannot escape the charge of being something of a *poseur*, and at times something of a phoney, which for him may mean the same thing. Once in twenty times his goods are genuine and joyously good (*Our Little Brown Brothers the Filipinos* is a classic example), but after eight volumes the Saroyan method shows no sign of change and appears to be incapable of further development.

Yet Saroyan is, I feel, important—not so much for what he has done, as for what he has indicated can be done. Saroyan has shown that the short story can be stripped of every shred of convention, turned inside out and upside down, and yet remain the short story. He has shown that it can exist not only without plot, which we knew already, without characterization, and without carefully created atmosphere, but without any of the other rules by which fictional life is projected through imagination. Saroyan's stories are the result of a kind of imaginative reportage; they are an embellished running commentary made by a man who stands at a street corner with a microphone in his hands and says, with pertinent or impertinent improvisation, what he feels about the life going past him. In his hands the method seems to have reached the limits of its immediate development; but it is possible that one day a writer will take that method, as Hemingway took the Stein method, and graft it on to a method more traditional and more exacting in its demand for imaginative form, and so produce a greater story.

Meanwhile every American short-story writer may congratulate himself on the moment in which he now lives. Behind him the conventions have been soundly and intelligently broken; he has been shown how, by turning inward, he may discover the foundations of that American tradition which a former generation sought to discover by turning outward; he has behind him a line of writers (Poe, Bierce, Crane, Jewett, Anderson, Hemingway, Faulkner, among others) who have set his country's short story on a level with the best in Europe, and in many cases higher than the best in Britain. Above all, he stands on the edge of fertile, almost virgin country; from a writing point of view the fertility of that country is limitless; for its exploitation he is offered a language already flexible but now, in the mouths of his countrymen, in a state of vigorous, exciting transition, rich with the smack of common poetry. While novelists turn back to re-create, in realistic-romantic terms, those sections of American history which their predecessors ignored (the Civil War, the Indian Wars, the wars with the British, the wars for gold), the American short-story writer is offered the golden chance of discovering the country and the people of his own time, and of interpreting those discoveries to himself and his fellow-men.

CHAPTER IX

LAWRENCE AND THE WRITERS OF
TO-DAY

UNLIKE the United States, England could never look
across the world and envy another country in which its
own language had through six centuries flowered into
literature. In that respect America was unique in the
world. British influences went directly and naturally
across the Atlantic, shaping the puritanical culture of
New England, setting formal traditional standards which
were carefully followed. But few, until American
literature began to free itself from these standards in the
nineteen-twenties, came back. Britain, standing at the extreme edge of Europe, took her influences from the mainland. Until the period after the First World War these
influences, as far as the short story was concerned, came
mainly from France and Russia ; but in the nineteen-
twenties the wind began to turn. Infiltration began to
make itself felt from America, and in a lesser degree
from Ireland, and it is for this reason that the contemporary short story of these two countries has been discussed before that of England.

In the immediate post-war years in Britain the gods of
the English short story were still, as I have already pointed
out, Kipling, Wells, O. Henry, Maugham, Galsworthy,

Conrad, and Henry James, all but two of whom had made and kept their reputations primarily as novelists. Until the arrival of Coppard and Katherine Mansfield no English writer, with the exception of Kipling, had made a reputation almost solely as a writer of stories ; and even Kipling had a vogue as a versifier which was itself a phenomenon. But by the middle nineteen-twenties Katherine Mansfield was dead, and Coppard had written the major part of his best work. Literature was either in the hands of the older, established, more commercial writers, of whom those listed above are good examples, or of a group of writers who, at the beginning of the war, had been men of sensibility, intellectual promise, and infinite hope, and who at the end of the war found themselves in a state of distrustful, bewildered nervous frustration, incapable of expressing themselves except by a kind of barren delicacy. Bloomsbury is their memorial.

A third group, too young to have borne arms, yet old enough to have seen the food queues, the marching men, and the silent crowds round the little altars of the back-street memorials and to have understood the meaning of it all, emerged from the war in a state of restless dislocation and inquiry. They saw behind them a shattered world : but it was not their world, and unlike the intellectuals of 1914 they could disclaim all share in having built it. The failure was not theirs ; they were confronted only with the resultant shambles, on which their elders still fondly hoped they would build noble and decent lives where religion, conservatism (or liberalism), social distinction, and reverence for the home, the body, and the Empire would still play a strong and honourable part. Unfortunately for that fond hope every accepted institution of the pre-war world had cracked foundations; the fabric of Church, home, morality, class distinction, and Empire was splitting, disrupted. "It was the age of the awkward question and the candid answer. . . . The intellectual or the anti-intellectual became the vogue, imagination and wonder ceased to find favour, and irony took the field over humour and sentiment. . . . Closely associated with this triumph of 'reason' occurred an outburst of interest in the rapidly developing science of analytical psychology. The novelist and the biographer re-examined human nature in the light of psycho-analysis, tracked down unconscious fears and desires, and traced them back to infantile complexes." [1]

In that vogue the work and influence of Aldous Huxley, Virginia Woolf, Joyce, and D. H. Lawrence were predominant; they were of the intermediate generation, not the young, but it was to them that the young were inevitably listening. All of them have a greater importance in a discussion on the novel than in one on the short story. The stories of Joyce have already been discussed; the stories of Virginia Woolf and Aldous Huxley are, beside their novels, negligible; but the stories of Lawrence are too large in both body and importance to be ignored.

Controversy has already dissected every bone in

[1] A. J. J. Ratcliff: *Prose of Our Time* (Nelson)

Lawrence's body and split every hair on his head, a performance to which I propose to add nothing. To consider Lawrence the short-story writer is a more straightforward task than that of considering him as a novelist, and for various reasons. The novel will suffer almost any kind of amplification of its theme, and Lawrence used it, to its repeated detriment, as a means of disseminating a personal gospel (" One has to be so terribly religious to be an artist ") that arose less from the head (" All scientists are liars ! ") than from the solar plexus (" I don't feel it *here* ! "). The statement of this gospel, since Lawrence was no thinker and was nothing if not " determined that all he produced should spring direct from the mysterious, irrational source of power within him," [1] was often windy and diffuse, but the novel contained it without bursting. Such a statement, preached in passionate and often hysterical terms incapable of modification (" I have often heard him say, indeed, that he was incapable of correcting " [2]), would destroy any short story by the simple process of suffocation. Lawrence, either intuitively or consciously, must have known this, and in consequence his stories are always an expression of a more direct, more controlled, and more objective art. In them Lawrence has no time to preach, to lose his temper, to go mystical, or to persuade the reader to listen to him by the doubtful process of shouting at the top of his voice and finally kicking him downstairs. Lawrence is for once bound to say what he has to say

[1] Aldous Huxley : intro. *Letters of D. H. Lawrence* (Heinemann)
[2] *Ibid.*

within reasonable, and even strict, limits of time and space. Ordinarily dictatorial, Lawrence is here dictated to by the form he has chosen. The results have little of that slobbering hysteria of the later novels ; they are again and again a superb expression of Lawrence's greatest natural gifts, sensibility, vision, a supreme sense of the physical (whether beautiful or ugly, human or otherwise), an uncanny sense of place, and a flaming vitality. Unobscured by hysteria, by the passion of theoretical gospels, these qualities shine through three-quarters of the forty stories that Lawrence wrote.

The publication of these stories began with *The Prussian Officer* in 1914. Lawrence, the son of a miner, had been brought up in one of those dreary rows of working-class houses that stand on the edge of the countryside they have robbed and desecrated. And here, in these first dozen stories, Lawrence aims to be nothing but the chronicler and interpreter of that life : a regional writer content to depict his own people. The vitality and authenticity of the pictures, strong with poetic realism, are striking. The eye recording them is clear, sharp, and vigorous, passionately observant, passionately responsive :

> The small locomotive engine, Number 4, came clanking, stumbling down from Selston with seven full wagons. It appeared round the corner with loud threats of speed, but the colt that it startled from among the gorse, which still flickered indistinctly in the raw afternoon, outdistanced it in a canter.

Ford Madox Hueffer seized on that passage as an indication of Lawrence's talent, and printed the story, *Odour of Chrysanthemums*, thus beginning Lawrence's career. He made no mistake ; the man who could describe this :

> Like a stream the path opened into azure shallows at the levels, and there were pools of bluebells, with still the green thread winding through, like a thin current of ice-water through the blue lakes.

could also describe this :

> She served the dinner and sat opposite him. His small bullet head was quite black, save for the whites of his eyes and his scarlet lips. It gave her a queer sensation to see him open his red mouth and bare his white teeth as he ate. His arms and hands were mottled black ; his bare, strong neck got a little fairer as it settled towards his shoulders, reassuring her. There was the faint indescribable odour of the pit in the room, an odour of damp, exhausted air.

There is no mistaking that. It is the voice of a man sensuously responsive to both beauty and ugliness ; to whom all life will be, in increasingly involved and violent terms, a conflict arising from that contradictory power of vision. But it is also the voice of a man with narrative powers, with the gift of unfolding words, of exciting curiosity : the gift of the story-teller. In the short stories this gift can be seen more clearly and more consciously at work than in the novels ; that spate of emotion, which Lawrence liked to call the expression of the dæmon in himself, is regulated, held in check, directed. The novel, as a form, never imposed this duty on Lawrence so rigidly ; in consequence the novels are often bad, shapeless, irritating in their insistent puerility and redundancy. To excuse this by saying that " he was determined . . . that the conscious intellect should never be allowed to come and impose, after the event, its abstract pattern of perfection " [1] is to relieve Lawrence of the obligation which imposes itself on every artist, whether he is writer or painter, film-producer or cabinet-maker. The reader, the audience, or the customer expects to be offered a finished article from which the chaotic chattering, the spoilt film, and the waste shavings of the workshop have been removed. Such self-denial was too much for Lawrence the novelist, who put the onus for the job on to a " dæmon within himself." He poured himself loosely on to the page and then, as always, protesting too much, declared, " They want me to have form . . . and I won't." From this impotent refusal to take hold of himself, to reject, shape, and direct the first molten outpouring of ideas, arises that feeling, so common in reading Lawrence, that the reader is being insulted. And this, it seems to me, is literally true. Much of Lawrence's work as a novelist treats the reader with contempt—a contempt comparable with that offered by the builder who, when the house is declared ready, is

[1] Aldous Huxley : *Letters of D. H. Lawrence* (Heinemann)

found to have left his rubble in every room and his scaffold still standing.

Later generations will react to the novels of Lawrence much as we now react to the novels of Hardy. The philosophical rumblings will date ; the wonderful pictures, the life directly projected, will remain. From such a test the short stories will emerge as the more durable achievement. In the earliest stories—*Daughters of the Vicar*, *The Shades of Spring*, the beautiful *Love Among the Haystacks*, and so on—the dæmon had not begun his dictation ; in the later stories—among which *The Man Who Loved Islands* and *The Fox* are masterpieces—the dæmon had either to be controlled or the story to lose its form as a story. In them Lawrence is still (and must be) obedient to one of his greatest gifts : that of narrative power, which in him is perhaps best described as the power of sustaining tension. Of that power, and its controlled use, *The Fox* and *The Man Who Loved Islands* are remarkable examples. In each such philosophy or moral as there is belongs to the bloodstream of the work, and is not a wild cloak flung on the body of it afterwards. And in each—and here is an important distinction that must be drawn between the novels and the stories—the principal male figure is someone other than Lawrence himself. Lawrence is again and again the hero, the ego, of the novels (*The White Peacock*, *The Trespasser*, *Sons and Lovers*, and various others), but in the stories this is rarely true. Lawrence, for these short periods, proves capable of devoting his objective attention to someone else. True, these males are often despicable (the officer in *The Prussian Officer*) or maliciously portrayed (the literary man in *The Man Who Loved Islands*), and have rarely that potent physical charm that characterizes Lawrence's own romanticized portraits of himself, but they are efforts, short but successful, in detached portraiture. That alone gives them a value which the novels often lack. They are impressed, but never oppressed, by the personality of their creator.

If Lawrence hated form and pretended to reject the idea of it in his own petulant way ("I won't"), it is nowhere obtruded, then, in the short stories. He proved amenable to whatever form the story imposed—long-short as in *The Fox*, *The Ladybird*, *The Captain's Doll*, and half a dozen others, or very short, as in *Second Best*, *Goose Fair*, *The Christening*, and others. Form here imposed on his genius the necessity for compression, and with fine results.

Clearly form was not Lawrence's primary contribution to the short story ; nor, as with Katherine Mansfield, oblique narration ; nor, as with Hemingway, a revaluation of style. Like Sherwood Anderson (with whom it is significant that he has often been compared) Lawrence turned his back on the conventionalized story in which most things hinged on artificially created problems or situations, and set to work to interpret his own people and the background of pit-heads, working-class houses, bluebell woods and hills, against which they lived. That, to Lawrence, must have seemed a very natural thing to do. Yet because Lawrence saw people as people his work was constantly stigmatized as shocking by the generation which had eagerly accepted the false and sadistic imperialism of Kipling and the scientific romancings of Wells. Yet Lawrence, being true to his own vision, will always be closer to life than either Kipling or Wells, and in that respect alone he set an example, as Anderson did in America, which a new decade of writers eagerly followed. Among the young short-story writers of 1940 you will find none, I think, who owe any important debt to Kipling or Wells; but you will find many who, as they depict the immediate life about them, have Lawrence to thank for the example.

I am not referring here to those who borrowed Lawrence's philosophy—they are innumerable and mostly forgotten—but to those who, in the post-war world of distrust and badly shaken values, found themselves, if they were writers, somewhere between prose and poetry. For them lyricism was not enough. Like Lawrence they were poets hit in the face by a clash of material events it was impossible to ignore. Once, the bluebell woods had been part of an untouched pastoral, undefiled, seemingly eternal; now the dirty houses, the miserable pitheads, lay across the vision. That exemplifies the situation in which the writers of the generation after Lawrence, even more than those of his own generation, found themselves. No poetry of great consequence came out of that generation (the thirties offer the new poets), but many short stories did.

The backbone of the English short story to-day is formed indeed largely by that generation—the generation born roughly between 1900 and 1910. It would be wrong to be too specific ; but to that decade belong V. S. Pritchett, L. A. G. Strong, Malachi Whitaker, H. A. Manhood, Leslie Halward, Arthur Calder-Marshall, Pauline Smith, James Hanley, Elizabeth Bowen, G. F. Green, Geraint Goodwin, Rhys Davies, T. O. Beachcroft, Dorothy Edwards, and the younger Irish writers already mentioned. These writers heard at every stage of their careers two parrot-cries : first, that the short story was unwanted and consequently unprinted and unread; secondly, that it was dead anyway, and that there had been no sign of its survival since the heyday of Kipling and Wells. If these things were true it is astonishing that these writers managed to make a reputation or even the semblance of a decent living. None of them is, I think, a plutocrat; none of them has the reputation of the late Edgar Wallace ; but they survive, live, and continue to write short stories—a fact which is in itself a vindication of their belief in the vitality of their art.

For they believed, naturally and rightly, that the short story was not dead. They believed that the short story had only in the last twenty years or so begun to face up to life closely. For years the gospel-cry of the short story had been plot, which no one had ever exactly defined, and which could be anything from a pattern to a clockwork apparatus that would strike an alarm at a given time. Yet when these writers looked back over a century of English fiction (and over French, American, and Russian fiction too), they must have been puzzled by how little of that kind of story remained. They drew the natural conclusion that the artificially plotted story cannot survive, and in support of it they could point to the persistent survival of the kind of story in which the reflection or interpretation of life and not the manipulation of it was of first importance. A writer of plot stories might succeed so long as he could keep up the supply of goods ; but death meant pretty quick oblivion. Yet somehow the stories of people like Gogol, Turgenev, Maupassant, Flaubert, Tchehov, Moore, Joyce, Crane, Bierce, and Gorki, among many others, managed to survive long after their creators were dead. Some stories, written to the same principle, had even survived for two thousand years or more, though the names of their creators were now unknown, doubtful, or forgotten. Plot had had no hand in the survival of *Susannah, Ruth, Judith,* or *The Prodigal Son.*

So in the 'twenties every writer of stories who broke with stereotyped tradition was of great importance, whatever his faults, if only as a source of encouragement. This was very true of Katherine Mansfield, Coppard, Joyce, Lawrence, and Sherwood Anderson. After them, writers followed in a stream. The tributaries ran wide. V. S. Pritchett and Ralph Bates wrote, like Hemingway, stories of Spain ; from the African veldt came a volume of tales, *The Little Karoo,* written by Pauline Smith with almost Biblical gravity ; in Wales, where the scene resembled Lawrence's Nottinghamshire, Rhys Davies wrote of the mining valleys, sharing Lawrence's love and hatred of his own people ; from Yorkshire came the little grim but delicate sketches of Malachi Whitaker ;

L. A. G. Strong wrote of the fishing-coasts of Ireland ; H. A. Manhood, in some ways resembling Coppard, wove a sort of tapestried poetry out of English country life ; James Hanley wrote of Liverpool, stevedores, and the sea ; Elizabeth Bowen and Dorothy Edwards wrote with delicate and rather serene irony of a more sophisticated middle-class or artistic life ; Arthur Calder-Marshall wrote of political life, Leslie Halward of bricklayers, plasterers, love in the front-room, and the Saturday football match in Birmingham ; T. F. Powys, Sylvia Townsend Warner, and David Garnett shaped the short story into a new form, that of realistic allegory ; Geraint Goodwin wrote of the little sour Welsh towns and the lovely Welsh border countryside.

All of them brought to the short story, among their own individual qualities, the realism and poetry it had sadly lacked. When it left their hands it was no longer a shoddy, manufactured stage-piece peopled by two-dimensional puppets. In form and effect it was close to, as it had in a sense supplanted, lyric poetry. Its characters, too, had a changed mode of behaviour. They no longer remained confined by the boundaries of the story, ticketed and docketed with conclusive labels. They tended to walk out of the story into independent existence. Towards this existence the reader made a greater contribution than ever before. The story now described less, but implied and suggested more ; it stopped short, it rendered life obliquely, or it was merely episodic ; so that the reader, if the value of the story was to be fully realized at all, had to supply the confirmation of his own experience, the fuller substance of the lightly defined emotion, and even the action between and after the episodes. The short story, in fact, moved nearer the film, and the two arts, rendering life largely by suggestion, brief episodes, picture-sequences, indirect narration, and the use of symbolism, developed together.

All this, however, was not a revolution in itself, but the result of a slow and rather disjointed process of revolution. In America, it seems to me, the short story has a continuous lineage in which a certain common heritage can be seen passing from one writer to another—Poe to Bierce, Bierce to Crane, Crane to Hemingway, Hemingway to Saroyan. But in England there is no common line of descent. We have no grounds for an equivalent of "We are all descended from Gogol's *Overcoat*." The short story kept its orphan status throughout the nineteenth century until at last Kipling and Wells gave it a name. It never knew a revolutionary hand.

And if to-day it stands freer, more fully emancipated, a livelier, more honest and more organically beautiful thing than before, it is more the result of the English aptitude for assimilating a wide variety of outside influences than of the revolutionary effort of one or more writers. The modern English short story owes more to Tchehov, Maupassant, and Hemingway than it does to any trio of its own native writers. What contemporary British writers of the short story are doing is excellent, but it is comparatively easy. To-day Mr. V. S. Pritchett's little masterpiece about a phoney religious revivalist, *The Saint*, is a piece of excellent ironical fun. But if only it had been written fifty years ago ! It is true that Mr. Pritchett would never again have been admitted to decent society, but the English short story would have been given a precedent beyond price. Substitute in this argument Lawrence's *The Fox*, Mrs. Whitaker's *Frost in April*, a story by James Hanley, Coppard, or Manhood, and the result would have been much the same. These stories would have been sources of derivation, and the English short story could have put forward the date of its proper tradition by half a century.

In the present-day short story one other thing is notable. Before Katherine Mansfield arrived, the short story had attracted no woman writer of importance here, though Mrs. Gaskell and Miss Ethel Colburn Mayne, an Irish writer, may be regarded as possible exceptions. After Katherine Mansfield the situation is very different. Though it may be only an incidental result of the larger movement of feminine emancipation, it is interesting that from 1920 onwards the list of distinguished women short-story writers grows, not only in Britain but in America, with astonishing rapidity. A projected anthology of the stories of women writers provided me, five or six years ago, with a preliminary list of nearly two hundred names. From this list the task (which proved impossible) was to select some thirty writers, among whom would certainly have been Malachi Whitaker, Elizabeth Bowen, Mary Arden, Kay Boyle, Dorothy Edwards, Pauline Smith, Katherine Mansfield, Winifred Williams, Katherine Ann Porter, Ruth Suckow, all of whom have brought distinction to the modern story. Women have contributed little to modern poetry, and it may be that the short story, which offers the nearest comparable form, has seemed to the responsive, intelligent, emotionally-urged woman writer the means of expression best adapted to her needs and those of the age. Whatever the reason, it is certain that the short story of to-day would be poorer without the contribution of these writers, whose only common defect is that, through ill-health or the inevitable family distractions, they do not write enough.

Meanwhile the short story, defying the premature notices of its death, has been given distinguished expression in a hitherto much-despised region. Welsh writers have learnt the lesson of Anderson and are beginning to write of their own people. Ten or fifteen years ago the only Welsh writers of consequence appeared to be Caradoc Evans and Rhys Davies, both of whom could be accused of whipping the poor dead Welsh colliery-chapel donkey very hard. Since that time Rhys Davies, though never shaking off the influence of Lawrence, has substituted for the rather erotic poetry of his earlier stories a quality of humour, partly robust, partly ironical, which has something in common with folk-lore. This gift, still not developed fully, is possibly the best part of himself. But his virtue is that, following Lawrence, he went back to his own people, to whom he remained tied by the equal bonds of sympathy and hatred. And for some years Davies showed—to an audience that was either not completely there or not completely listening—that there was, in Wales, a life as remote from life in England as the life in the Ohio valleys was remote from the life of New York. By his example Davies urged its re-discovery. That re-discovery was delayed by two factors : first, by the long economic depression, which paralysed so much of Welsh life and inevitably sterilized the little artistic impulse that remained ; and secondly, by English prejudice, which eagerly grasps at any interpretation of Irish life, even though it springs directly from hatred of England, but which rejects the corresponding interpretation of Welsh life with blank or sour indifference. An Irish play in London is an event ; a Welsh play [1] gets its London production, if it gets it at all, in a back-street little theatre, and is then shipped back to Wales in the next empty coal-truck. This is true also of Welsh novels ; truer of short stories. In defence of the English attitude it must be said that Welsh writers, depressed, appalled, and angered by that sour parochial gloom which the very sensitive feel as they cross the border, used for many years a stereotyped pattern, of which colliery valleys, chapels, meanness, avarice, the dole, the sacred front room, revivals and revolts and love-in-the-entry were the inevitable parts. Readers began to know what to expect ; and they had a right to expect, if they were to be interested in Welsh literature at all, a change of mood.

There is no doubt that this change has come. In the *Best Short Stories, 1940 : English*, for example, no less than one-third of the chosen stories are Welsh, an event

[1] With exceptions like Mr. Emlyn Williams's *The Corn is Green*, and the film of Mr. Richard Llewellyn's *How Green is My Valley*

for which there is no precedent in the twenty-five years of that series. Margiad Evans, Rhys Davies, Geraint Goodwin, Edgar Howard, Glyn Jones, Gwyn Jones, and Alun Lewis contribute these stories, most of which are taken from *The Welsh Review*, itself a proof of the vitality of an independent Welsh literature. To this list should be added the names of Dylan Thomas, who has brought to the dream-fantasy story a vocabulary of lavish poetic delirium by which the short story makes yet another turn of development (see such a story as *The Orchards*) ; and of Kate Roberts, who has written a series of remarkable stories in Welsh and who has the distinction of being, like Tchehov, intelligently and beautifully translated.

In the work of all these writers, from the dark and rather wooden melodramas of Margiad Evans to the quiet realism of Kate Roberts, there is a quality that may perhaps best be described as illumination. The light of poetic imagination is turned on Wales with revelations of astonishing beauty, colour, drama, truth ; the work of Glyn Jones, closely imitative of that of Dylan Thomas, has the quality of pure pastoral. Twenty years ago it would have seemed impossible that Wales, popularly considered a country of sour stone, hideous defamation, and colourless mountains, should have yielded literature for which perhaps a close precedent is the Impressionist period of painting. For Welsh writers seem to have made precisely the discovery that French painters made almost a hundred years ago ; they have decided to paint in the open air. The results, strong and sometimes lavishly coloured, sometimes fierily imaginative, always close to life, are seen at their best in the work of Welsh short-story writers, who now occupy in the English short story the place occupied ten years or so ago by the Irish. In contrast to the present state of Irish literature the rebirth of Welsh literature is a remarkable thing. The Irish short story is standing still ; and it remains a nice piece of irony that, whereas much of the best in modern Irish literature emerged directly from the clash of hatred against England, the reborn independent Eire has produced not a tenth of that literature, of comparable quality. The Irish thrive on the romanticism of old feuds and the realism of new ; left alone, they slip into stagnation, fed upon in turn by the mild decadent air of Irish isolation.

Towards Wales, then, the English short story may perhaps begin to look for a new influence. This may be small, but it is unquestionably vital, and periodically the English short story shows itself in need of some outside measure, rather than an influence, by which it can check the progress of its own achievement, reassess things, and then again go forward. It is somewhere near that position to-day. The period of the Mansfield story is at an end ; the curve of Tchehov's influence declines ; we have learnt as much as is good for us to learn from Hemingway, though the newer Hemingway stories of Spain will repay, for sheer clean craftsmanship, every moment of study. The new war inevitably walls off, as it were, the old era. The story of tranquil, reflective surface, in which the currents of emotion move out of sight, belongs to that era primarily ; it will always have its place and be capable, in the right hands, of beautiful and significant development, but the new era of terror and dislocation, of the bomb in the home, of the battle in the stratosphere, will —and is bound to—demand a change of form. If the story of the past twenty years has been close to the lyric, the short story of the next twenty years may move, or be forced to move, nearer to dramatic poetry. I say may advisedly, with caution, since literary movements are quite beyond prophecy. But move the short story must, somewhere. It will be hit, undoubtedly, by the backwash of romanticism after the tide of the present war is spent ; the era in which people will want to be amused, not reminded, and in which realism (or whatever it is then called) will be at a considerable discount. But the vitality of its progress will depend then, as always, on its courage in scaling what Miss Elizabeth Bowen calls " peaks of common experience " and of moving " past an altitude line into poetry."

Chapter X

PROSPECT

Form and method are things which sooner or later disturb any discussion on fiction, whether short or long. Yet a man writes, as Tchehov pointed out, as he must and as he will, and there all discussion of form and method might end. For the most revolutionary method probably seems, to its creator, the most natural : hence the painful surprise which awaits generations of writers who, setting down things as they see and feel them, find they have rudely shocked the public, bringing down on their heads angry charges of godlessness and immorality. A writer's method is, on a final assessment, himself. Yet if he is a writer of stories or a writer of poems he must accept the imposition and limitation of form. In choice of subject, like the novelist, he is free ; unlike the novelist, who is so lightly held by restrictions that he can express himself in any length between a hundred and fifty pages and a thousand and five hundred and even in several volumes (*cf.* Dorothy Richardson's *Miriam* chronicle in nine volumes, or Proust's *Remembrance of Things Past*), the short-story writer and the poet must accept certain restrictions of length. For centuries the poet even had to accept a certain numerical restriction in the matter of syllables ; the sonnet in particular held him

in chains ; the heroic couplet threatened to make a
mockery of his art. The short story, not so rigidly
confined as a sonnet yet superficially more restricted than
a novel, stands nearer the drama than either. It is at
once restricted, yet free ; its range of time, place, and
movement is necessarily limited, and like the drama
it is forced back on the use of suggestion, implied action,
indirect narration, and symbolism to convey what might
otherwise be conveyed by a plain catalogue of solid
words. Spectacular dramatists, having nothing to say,
often remedy this defect by expanding the stage until it
can contain the world outside, even to the accommoda-
tion of a railway train or a Mississippi steamboat. The
cinema finally defeats them. But the short story has
no need for such cardboard manipulation ; it is free to
suggest the railway train or describe the railway train,
as it will ; it is free in a sense that the drama is never
free—it may describe, in natural detail, the things that
may never happen on the stage : an undraped woman,
a road crash, an air-battle, and countless others. Or it
is free of description at all, and may rely, as Hemingway's *Hills Like White Elephants* relies, almost entirely
on conversation and the ability of the reader to draw the
appropriate descriptive and emotional conclusions from
that conversation. Or there may be no conversation,
but only description, and indirect description at that. Or
there may be description and conversation, both direct
and suggestive, with a coherence of action and an
obedience to the unities such as would satisfy the most
academic dramatist. In short, once the short story has

accepted a certain light restriction of length (say between a hundred and fifty words, which is roughly the length of *The Prodigal Son*, and fifteen thousand words, which is somewhere near the length of Tolstoy's *Family Happiness*), the short-story writer is the freest of all artists in words : far freer than the dramatist, infinitely freer than the poet, and in reality far freer than the novelist, since he is offered a wealth of subjects which it is unprofitable, undignified, or otherwise not worth the novelist's while to touch.

During the last hundred years it is the realization of this freedom that has altered the whole character of the written short story. In Poe's time the short story is seen as an entertaining but extremely restricted form ; it had little to do with the world, and the countless subjects in it, beyond the narrow limits of pathological fantasy. In 1820 stories about a bricklayer's labourer or the mocking of a religious revivalist would have been either squibs or bombshells, equally impossible. As the century went on this poverty of subject continued to be an inseparable part of the English short story, though there was no parallel for it in Russia, France, or America. When the short story appeared it resembled, mostly, a précis of the novel. England possessed neither a Maupassant nor a Tchehov, to whom no kind of person or subject was forbidden material ; and until their influence permeated the stiff parochial hide with which public opinion surrounded fiction, as it surrounded drama, no English short story of consequence existed. Thanks partly to this parochialism, which swooned with horror at Tess, burnt *Jude the Obscure*, destroyed *The Rainbow*, and even now sends horrified protests to editors of periodicals and authors everywhere, the English short story suffered fifty years of arrested development in the learning of the simple lesson that to the short-story writer, even more than to the dramatist and novelist, all subjects are legitimate and accordingly free. That lesson is part of the consciousness of every serious writer of stories to-day, with the result that the range and importance of the contemporary English short story is greater than it has ever been.

This breaking down of illogical moral prejudice against subject—murder was always for some reason a splendid and legitimate subject, plain natural physical love a blue horror—is therefore as important as any development in form. Because of it, expression has been made freer, more direct, and an increase in flexibility is probably the most consistent development during the last hundred years. Inessential paraphernalia has dropped away, the casual explanatory lead-up of the club arm-chair has gone (" Four of us were having a sundowner when Carruthers, apropos of nothing, remarked," etc.), the moral-issue opening and the pompous philosophical statement have also gone (" We are all creatures of perverse circumstance, tossed willy-nilly by fate, ever cruel, but if ever there was a person who less deserved the arrows of outrageous fortune it was Edith Carstairs ") and with them the sermon ending (" It is not for us to judge. But I believe if ever there was a good man it was Roger Carmichael," etc.). These are extreme and stupid examples which look pretty silly now, but for years they were part of the accepted heavy mediocrity of a certain type of English story. Fortunately that very method has given to a small group of writers a delightful opportunity for the creation of a type of story which, just as much as *The Killers*, *The Saint*, and *The Daring Young Man on the Flying Trapeze*, would have been something of a revolution a century ago. Burlesque has been beautifully handled by Wodehouse in England, and by Thurber, Damon Runyon, and Stephen Leacock among others in America. It is interesting, and I think significant, that at least two of these writers are, like Lewis Carroll, very serious-minded gentlemen in an academic way, and it would be a mistake to suppose that because they write with levity their subjects and their treatments are not to be taken seriously. The satirical art of Leacock, as of the others, offers delicious study :

It was a wild and stormy night on the West Coast of Scotland. This, however, is immaterial to the present story, as the scene is not laid in the West of Scotland. For the matter of that the weather was just as bad on the East Coast of Ireland.

Such stuff is an essential, salutary part of the story's development. It prevents the story from growing obese, windy, self-satisfied. It applied the same medicine as Hemingway himself applied in the self-satirical *Torrents of Spring*. It is laughing not so much at life as at literature, which is an excellent thing. For there is always

218

a danger that a highly individual style, like that of Lawrence, Tchehov, Hemingway, or Caldwell, will become the subject of unconscious parody, or self-parody, or both, by which the essential vitality of the influence is killed. For example, the extent of the imitation of Hemingway's flat style has not only robbed the method of much usefulness, but has even forced on Hemingway a certain return to conservatism of style, by which he saves himself from the charge of self-parody. This is notable in some of the later stories, making Hemingway look almost traditional.

If I have hitherto said little of form, in a chapter primarily intended to be a summary of that subject, it is for several reasons. First, any real examination of the story's developments of shape would involve the dissection of almost every story written. No two stories are alike ; no two methods. Many of what seem to be the best or most significant developments have been discussed earlier in the book. Moreover I have no prejudices ; the story is the thing, and can be written in an infinite number of ways. There are stories whose contents can be summarized, neatly, in the form of anecdote ; there are stories which are themselves nothing more than anecdotes ; stories in which development is plotted by abrupt sequences of action, counter-action, and climax ; stories which glance off life, obliquely, at a tangent ; stories which are cut out of life, with edges still raw ; stories which are mere episodes, stopping short, final significance withheld ; stories which are allegorical, adventurous, reflective, purely pictorial, ingenious, psychological ; stories which are pieces of flat reportage ; stories which say everything by the process of appearing to say nothing at all. All are acceptable ; all are common parts of the development of the modern story. Critical jargon will talk about them and round them all, but critical jargon has no word for that quality, which might be described as balance, which is the expression of the instinctive part of the writer's self. A story must, so to speak, be weighed in the hands, to a fine and intuitive test. Its balance will collapse under a superfluous sentence, even a superfluous word. To see a writer building up his tale, piece by piece, as one builds up a toy tower of match-sticks, and to feel that he knows both instinctively and consciously which match-stick must be last and exactly when the tower will bear no more, is an experience which can become, also, a general critical test of form. For the story which passes the application of that simple test, whether it is a story of smart plot, subtle inflections, action or symbolism, fact or fantasy, or anything else, may be said to have passed all tests. And as prime examples of that balanced perfection, which gives the reader the incomparable feeling of being slightly lifted off the earth, I would say that certain Biblical stories, notably *Ruth*, *The Prodigal Son*, *Susannah*, and *Jonah*, certain stories of Hans Andersen, notably *The Princess and the Pea*, and a few modern stories such as *Boule de Suif*, Tchehov's little sketch *The Beauties*, Gorki's *Twenty-six Men and a Girl*, Bierce's *A Horseman in the Sky*, and Joyce's *The Dead* are, with a very few others, supreme.

As long as there are writers who can successfully apply that test of balance, the short story, in no matter what form, will survive. Meanwhile, what else contributes to its survival, in England especially, as an artistic form ? Precious little, I fear, except the writer himself. To wait for the public to reveal a sign of artistic courage about the short story is to die of paralysis. The reader who, at the public library, is given a book of short stories under the impression that the book is a novel still feels a strong justification for a suit against the librarian for false pretences. The most successful short-story writer of a serious kind in England to-day probably never sells more than five thousand copies a time, the least successful not more than a hundred. There are few magazines devoted entirely to the short story, yet some good work has been done along lines similar to *New Writing*. Half a dozen papers nobly struggle to print a story in each issue ; the rest are slaves to the most ephemeral form of prose expression, after topical news, that exists—namely the comment on topical news. Nor are the patrons of culture much help. England has three literary prizes of any consequence, none of which, so far as I can discover, has ever been awarded to a volume of stories, though one was once awarded to a short story called *Lady into Fox*, thanks to the ingenuity of its creator, who very wisely called it a novel. Philanthropic millionaires never seem to consider that a modest trust of £10,000 would provide two handsome literary prizes every year as a contribution to the slight advancement of culture ; in England there are no Pulitzer prizes, no O. Henry Memorial Award.

The result is that writers are forced into Broadcasting House, to work as manuscript readers for publishers, agents, and film companies, to scratch for odd guineas as reviewers, to write detective stories, advertisements, and indeed anything except the things they want to write. Poverty, as Mr. Somerset Maugham has with characteristic good sense pointed out, can be for the writer a powerfully destructive influence; the garret is a romantic and cynical cliché.

" For the future lies," as Miss Elizabeth Bowen has said, " not with the artist only; the reader and the critic have a share in it. If the short story is to keep a living dignity, and is not to be side-tracked into preciousness, popular impatience on the one hand and minority fervour on the other will have to be kept in check. The present state of the short story is, on the whole, healthy : its prospects are good."

Towards the better realization of that last point much of this volume has been directed. More short-story writers are to-day writing in England and America, and moreover writing better stories, than ever before. That fact is no accident. A particular artistic form does not flourish in a particular age because of a happy accident, but because certain cultural, inventive, revolutionary, or popular forces combine to stimulate its growth : so that finally, perhaps, it becomes the most necessary and natural expression of the age. This was notably true of the drama in Elizabethan times, the heroic couplet in the eighteenth century, the novel in the nineteenth century, and in a lesser but increasing way is true of the short story to-day.

The war of 1914–18 prepared the ground for a new story ; the intermediate period of distrust and dislocation fostered it ; and it would not surprise me very much if the literature of the second war, and its inevitable aftermath of still more distrustful dislocation, found in the short story the essential medium for whatever it has to say. For it is certain that, as Hemingway has proved of Spain, if no other good comes out of wars, stories will.

INDEX

Adam and Eve and Pinch Me (Coppard), 134.
Alton Locke (Kingsley), 102.
Amateurs, 7–9.
American Civil War, 53, 67–69.
American short stories, 46–71; competitive, 8; indigenous material, 26, 164–65; nineteenth-century writers, 36; no class-barriers, 48, 64; humour, 49, 64; affected by prudery, 49; lineage, 207; arid period, 71; lack of culture, nineteenth century, 72–73; renaissance, 161, 163–93; Hemingway, 167–78; subsequent writers, 179–93; modernists since 1925, 180 *et seq.*; women writers, 180; names, 180–81.
American Short Stories of the Nineteenth Century, 48.
Andersen, Hans, 220.
Anderson, Sherwood, 18, 23–24, 27, 133–34; *Winesburg Ohio*, 35; regionalism, 52; and Stephen Crane, 71; parodied, 90; pioneer, 161, 163–67, 178.
Andreyev, Leonid, 95.
Aspects of Literature (Middleton Murry), 84*n*.
Austen, Jane, 57, 58, 59, 101.

Baltimore, 26, 28.
Balzac, Honoré de, 34, 35.
Bates, H. E., aim, 10–12, 14, 25; ignores own stories, 11–12; compared with Tchehov, 11; *The Short Story*, by, 14*n*.
Bates, Ralph, 205.
Beachcroft, T. O., 204.
Beer, Thomas, 65, 65*n*.
Bennett, Arnold, 35, 105, 132,

147; debt to Dickens and Turgenev, 44.
Best British Short Stories, 1927, 121*n*. (For other collections, British and American, see under O'Brien, E. J.)
Bible, The, "short stories" in, 13, 205, 220; influence on Hemingway, 173, 173*n*.
Bierce, Ambrose, 36, 47; American Civil War, 53; qualities, 52–56, 67, 70.
Black Monk, The, 82.
Bliss (Katherine Mansfield), 125.
Boule de Suif (Maupassant), 9, 35, 73, 74, 93.
Bowen, Miss Elizabeth, 204; *Faber Book of Modern Stories*, 14 and 14*n.*, 17*n.*, 21*n.*, 150*n.*; views, 16, 21, 100; on Jane Austen, 65; own stories, 206; on future of short story, 213, 222.
Brave New World (Aldous Huxley), 179.
Bride Comes to Yellow Sky, The (Crane), 70.
Broadcasting, 222.
Brontë, Charlotte, 35, 43, 101.
Brooke, Rupert, 123.
Burlesque in fiction, 218.
Burns, Robert, 84.
Butler, Samuel (1835–1902), *The Way of All Flesh*, 41, 83; iconoclast, 96, 125.

Caine, Hall, 115, 118.
Cakes and Ale (Maugham), 143–144.
Calder-Marshall, Arthur, 204, 206.
Caldwell, Erskine, 180, 183–84.